GLOBE QUARTOS

THOMAS HEYWOOD

THE WISE WOMAN OF HOXTON

First printed: London, 1638

This edition prepared by Sonia Massai

GLOBE EDUCATION

NICK HERN BOOKS

LONDON

www.nickhernbooks.co.uk

GLOBE QUARTOS

This edition of *The Wise Woman of Hoxton*
first published in Great Britain
as a paperback original in 2002
by Nick Hern Books Limited
14 Larden Road, London W3 7ST

in association with

Globe Education
Shakespeare's Globe, New Globe Walk
London SE1 9DT

Printed by CLE Print Ltd, St Ives, Cambs PE27 3LE

A CIP catalogue record for this book is available from
the British Library

ISBN 1 85459 707 8

PREFACE

Over 400 plays written between 1567 and 1642 have survived in print. Few are now read and even fewer are performed. In 1995 Globe Education initiated a 30-year project to stage readings with professional casts of all the surviving texts so that audiences may once again hear plays by Barnes, Haughton, Shirley, Wilkins *et al*.

In 1997 Mark Rylance, Artistic Director of Shakespeare's Globe, included full productions of Beaumont and Fletcher's *The Maid's Tragedy* and Middleton's *A Chaste Maid in Cheapside* as part of the Globe Theatre's opening season. Over 30,000 people came to hear and see the two plays.

The popularity of the readings and the productions prompted Globe Education to approach Nick Hern to publish the texts being revived at the Globe to enable more people to read, study and, ideally, to produce them. Developments in computer typesetting have enabled editions to be published economically and quickly as *Globe Quartos*.

The first *Globe Quartos* were edited in 1998 by Nick de Somogyi. In 1999 an Editorial Board, composed of David Scott Kastan, Gordon McMullan and Richard Proudfoot, was established to oversee the series.

Globe Education is indebted to all those who have helped to give new life to old plays: production teams, actors, audiences, directors, editors, publishers and readers.

Patrick Spottiswoode
Director, Globe Education

EDITORIAL BOARD'S PREFACE

The aim of the series is to make once more available English plays of the late sixteenth and early seventeenth centuries that have long been out of print in affordable form or have been available to readers only in scholarly editions in academic libraries. The *Globe Quartos* texts are based on the most reliable surviving forms of these plays (usually the first printed editions). These have been fully edited and modernised so as to make them easily usable by actors and readers today. Editorial correction and emendation are undertaken where required by the state of the original. Extra stage directions added by editors and needed to make the action clear are enclosed in square brackets. Apostrophes in verse speeches indicate elision of syllables and reflect the metrical pattern of the line. Prefatory matter includes notes from the director or co-ordinator of the production or reading of the play at the Globe and a brief factual introduction by the editor. Glossarial notes (keyed to the text by line numbers) explain difficult or obsolete usages and offer brief comment on other points of interest or obscurity. Departures from the wording of the original are recorded in textual notes that identify the source of corrections or editorial emendations. The opening page of the text in the original on which the edition is based is reproduced in reduced facsimile. Extra material relevant to the understanding of the play may occasionally be included in an Appendix.

ACKNOWLEDGEMENTS

I would like to thank the general editors of the Globe Quarto Series, Thomas L. Berger, David Scott Kastan and Gordon McMullan, for giving me the opportunity to edit this long-neglected comedy. I am *mille et mille modis* indebted to Thomas L. Berger, whose expertise as an established editor of early modern drama has greatly benefited the present edition. I particularly appreciated being guided through a wide range of reference sources, which substantially improved my appreciation of the topical and theatrical qualities of this play text. Gordon McMullan's generous contribution as general editor and scrupulous proof-reader has proved crucial, especially during the final stages of the project. Several other colleagues and friends have played a role in the preparation of this edition. Special thanks to: P. Pattenden and Eva Griffith, who provided information on the early stages of Heywood's career as a student in Cambridge and as a young dramatist in London; Jonathan Hope, who advised me on how to modernise a time expression in 5.1; David Steel, who pointed out an intriguing connection between the Gunpowder Plot and Hoxton; and Richard Proudfoot, Derek Hughes, Susan Reed, Giles Mandelbrote and Cosimo Pacciani, who helped me with the "slippery" Greek and Latin used by Sir Boniface and Sencer in 2.2 and 4.1.

Sonia Massai

A Note from the Co-Ordinator

Staged Reading – Globe Education (4 November 2001)

My experience with rarely performed works by Elizabethan dramatists is that they play much better than they read. This is especially true with a piece in such a strong farcical tradition as *The Wise Woman of Hoxton*. In order to appreciate the theatricality of the piece, the reader needs to bear in mind that dialogue grows out of a specific set of circumstances, and so should picture each scene with consideration of who is on stage and where in the geography of the play the scene is taking place. This is often explicit in the stage directions but when preparing these plays for performance I sometimes find that I have to make some educated guesses.

On the page, *The Wise Woman of Hoxton* is a well-observed city comedy embracing various social types with some neat turns of phrase which serve as pointers that encourage vivid characterisation. There is a rich array of young dissipated gallants; members of an aspirant merchant-class; tradesmen and artisans; the nouveaux riches and newly ennobled aristocrats; irate fathers, with comical concerns for their social position, all pushing ungainly daughters towards dubious suitors. Given the fact that the women's parts would originally have been played by men, I always encourage actresses not to be afraid of the grotesque and to be aware of the transvestite double-entendres that would have been obvious to a contemporary audience. With the introduction of the Wise Woman – who gives herself airs and graces as a great Madam, while being nothing more than a back-street abortionist, a brothel-keeper, and a purveyor of some of the most extraordinary medical remedies in Elizabethan theatre – we find a unique forum for an intermingling of these vying and varying worlds to the great delight of the audience.

When working on *The Wise Woman of Hoxton* with actors, I find myself drawing on the relationships and characterisations in Shakespeare as a useful way of illuminating the dramatic situations of his contemporaries. The question of whose character derives from whom is often an ongoing matter for debate in rehearsal, and a useful shorthand guide. As in *Love's Labour's Lost* we relish being immersed in a world of immature men who follow a rocky course throughout the play towards maturity and marriage. We first encounter our heroes in a huddle such as we find in the court of Navarre. As in *All's Well that End's Well*, there are exchanges where men try to wear down women's defences and, just as in Shakespeare, we have a heroine engaged on an obsessive quest to win back an inconstant absconder. With the character of Luce we are reminded of Rosalind disguising herself as a boy to achieve her objectives, and, as with Rosalind, we are compelled, during a high point in the drama, to process the fact that she is a girl, dressed up as a boy pretending to be a girl.

The heart of *The Wise Woman of Hoxton* is the bittersweet romance of Chartley and Luce, but there is also immense delight to be had from the Sencer/Gratiana and Boyster/Luce 2 sub-plots. Boyster, the blunt dullard, and Sencer, the mercurial shape-shifter, offer rich opportunities in performance. Harringfield doesn't get a girl but provides the function of a Benvolio, a peacemaker, the reconciler of his friends' differences and facilitator of their ambitions, and his charm does not go unnoticed by glad-eyed Gratiana

Reality is routinely strained in situation comedy, but, in order for the infernal machinery of farce to work, a willing suspension of disbelief is required on entering a world of mistaken identities, coincidence and impenetrable disguises. Situations are set up and played out in front of our eyes; we are soon ahead of the game and we shortly come to appreciate how the farcical mechanism of the play works. Despite its technical structure, it is a warm-hearted piece in which good nature is seen to prevail in the last scene where Chartley is systematically thwarted in his attempts to squirm out of one compromising position after another; the Wise Woman's desire for revenge is satisfied and Luce's constancy is deservedly recognised.

So with these thoughts, I hope readers take pleasure in this romantic city comedy and allow themselves to be conjured into a benevolent universe in which, despite all the intervening diversions and subversions, honour, modesty and the other moral virtues are ultimately rewarded.

Alan Cox

THE WISE WOMAN OF HOXTON

Cast of the play, which was co-ordinated by Alan Cox at the Globe Education Centre on 4 November 2001

Robin Chartley	James Wallace
Boyster	James Chalmers
Sencer	Alex Harcourt-Smith
Haringfield	Jean-Paul van Cauwelaert
Luce	Alexis Karne
Luce's Father	Heathcote Williams
Joseph	Ewan Watson
Old Master Chartley	Sam Cox
Giles	Andrew Watson
A Serving-man	Andrew Watson
Sir Harry	Bryan Robson
Gratiana	Katarina Olsson
Tabor	Duncan Wisbey
Sir Boniface	Liam McKenna
The Wise Woman of Hoxton	Jeanne Hepple
Luce 2	Rebecca Palmer
A Countryman	Andrew Watson
A Kitchen-Maid	Krista Spampinato
Citizen's Wife	Esther Elizabeth

Other parts played by members of the Company

EDITOR'S INTRODUCTION

Thomas Heywood (c.1574-1641), actor, playwright and man of letters, famously claimed to have had 'either an entire hand, or at least a maine finger' in the 'penning' of two hundred and twenty plays by 1633. Heywood's connection with the world of the public playhouses in London is first documented by an entry in Henslowe's *Diary*, which dates back to 1596. According to the *Diary*, Henslowe lent his actors thirty shillings for the purchase of 'Hawodes booke'. By 1598, Heywood was a share-holding member of Henslowe's company, the Admiral's Men, who performed at the Rose Theatre in Southwark until 1600, when Henslowe built the Fortune Theatre. By 1602, Heywood had moved to Worcester's Men, who, after touring the country for over ten years, had recently merged with Oxford's Men to become the third London company. Upon the accession of James I, Heywood's company became the Queen's Men. It was with the Queen's Men at the Curtain Theatre in Shoreditch that Heywood premiered his masterpiece, *A Woman Killed with Kindness*, in 1603.

Although printed in 1638, there are reasons to believe that *The Wise Woman of Hoxton* was also performed by the Queen's Men around the time when the company moved from the Curtain to The Red Bull, a newly built theatre in Clerkenwell which would house them permanently until 1617. F. G. Fleay identifies the play with a comedy called *How to Learn of a Woman to Woo*, which was presented before the King on 20 December 1604. Fleay's identification would seem to be disproved by two allusions to the Gunpowder Plot (1605) at 3.2.40 and 5.2.129. However, given that the play was in a "state of composition" until it was printed in 1638, these two allusions could have been added at a later stage,. The first one, for example, adds humour and topicality to a passage which would still make sense without it. The second allusion is the only verse line in a prose speech spoken by Chartley, who tends to use prose rather than verse. Besides, this verse line opens Chartley's speech and, as with 3.2.40, it could be taken out without affecting the overall economy of the exchange. Although a date of composition cannot be definitively established, suggestive internal evidence confirms that the play must have been written shortly after the beginning of the seventeenth century. The play clearly belongs to a peculiar group of plays which flourished on the London stage around 1602-3, and which focus on the character of a Griselda-like heroine. Mrs Arthur in Heywood's *How a Man May Choose a Good Wife from a Bad* (1602) and Helena and Mariana in Shakespeare's *All's Well that Ends Well* (1602) and *Measure for Measure* (1603/4) are among the best-known examples. Even more suggestive are references to plays which were popular around the turn of the seventeenth century: *Jack Drum's Entertainment* (publ. 1601) and a lost play called *Dick Cutting*, which Heywood himself revised around 1602, are mentioned at 2.2.132-33 and 2.1.144 (see glossarial notes for more details). Besides, a line spoken by Chartley at 5.2.178-9, 'neither married man, widower nor bachelor' echoes very closely a line which also occurs in the last scene of *Measure for Measure*, when the Duke puzzles over Mariana's status, as being 'neither maid, widow nor wife' (5.1.178-9).

The title-page of the first Quarto edition published in 1638 may attest to the play's popularity. The play was apparently acted 'sundry times' and 'with great applause'. There are, however, no records of later revivals. The play was reprinted twice in the second half of the nineteenth century (Pearson, 1874; Verity, 1888) but aroused no special critical interest. The exposition of the Wise Woman as a charlatan has traditionally encouraged a comparison of the play with Ben Jonson's *The Alchemist*. The conflicting views expressed by nineteenth- and twentieth-century critics on this issue give a sense of the slow but steady process of rediscovery enjoyed by this neglected comedy. Whilst A. W. Verity claims that 'mentioning it in the same breath as Jonson's *The Alchemist* would be ridiculous' (1888: xiii), A. C. Clark argues that *The Wise Woman of Hoxton* 'lays bare the tricks of all manner of pretenders to wisdom' as effectively as its popular Jonsonian counterpart (1931: 246). Even T. S. Eliot, who regards Heywood as one of the 'dimmest figures' among his contemporaries, admits that in *The Wise Woman of Hoxton* 'he succeeds with something not too far below Jonson to be comparable to that master's work' (1963 [1931], 101). Since the late twentieth century, critical attitudes have changed dramatically. Far from reading the play as a morally loaded attempt to expose the Wise Woman as a charlatan, Jean Howard devotes a section of *The Stage and Social Struggle in Early Modern England* (1994) to the play and identifies the Wise Woman's power with theatricality itself.

The last scene powerfully illustrates Howard's analysis, according to which 'power is shown to lie with the theatrically skilful, and in this play the most theatrically skilful figures are women' (1994: 89). The Wise Woman's plan to expose Chartley by arranging a rendezvous with the London Luce, which is secretly watched by his victims (5.2), is representative of the power the Wise Woman derives from manipulating reality theatrically. The complex staging required by 5.2 reminds one of the eavesdropping scene in Shakespeare's *Love's Labour's Lost* (4.3). Despite her remarkable theatrical skills, the Wise Woman is outwitted by another woman, Luce 2, who, while disguised as Jack, rises to the challenge of a double bluff by pretending to be the London Luce whom Chartley is convinced he has wed. If none of the other characters realises that Chartley's newly-wed is really a boy, no one, including the Wise Woman, realises that Jack is really a girl.

The seemingly awkward naming of two central characters as Luce and Luce 2 is in fact a clever device that heightens the farcical intrigue, as in 1.2, when the jilted Luce catches up with her betrothed only to hear him rehearse his vows to marry another Luce the following day. On a different level, this device attracts our attention to the obvious differences between the two characters. Despite her association with the Wise Woman, who calls her 'one of my daughters' in 2.1, the London Luce is virtuous because ultimately passive and obedient. Luce 2 is transgressive because she is extremely resourceful and ultimately deceptive. What is remarkable about the ending, which in contemporary comedies normally restores patriarchy through the institution of marriage, is that Luce 2 is the only woman who gets the husband she has actively pursued since the opening of the play. The supremacy of the Wise Woman over Chartley and the comic resolution granted to the romantic quest of Luce 2 challenge the three male suitors' perception of women as precious commodities, not unlike the variety of desirable objects available from the Exchange or Cheapside.

The radical quality of this comedy never undermines its light-hearted tone. Through a clever mixture of prose and verse, Heywood conjures some of his favourite stock characters – the dissolute youth, the pedantic schoolmaster, the foolish old father – setting them against the bustling streets of an early seventeenth-century London lined with taverns, gambling-houses and goldsmiths' shops. The colourful setting is more than a backdrop to action and dialogue, however. By mentioning other 'reverend matrons' and fortune-tellers in Pepper Alley, Coldharbour, Clerkenwell Green, Westminster and the Bankside (2.1), the Wise Woman places Hoxton and her own activities "on the map". Similarly, when the foppish Chartley specifies that he rode 'out of Holborn' and then 'turn'd by Islington' to visit Luce in Hoxton (5.2), thus preferring the fashionable old highway to the grimmer route out of Bishopsgate or Moorgate, he is making a self-conscious statement (for more details, see Glossarial Note 5.2.89). Even the amusing competition Sir Harry sets up between Sir Boniface, the pedantic schoolmaster who insists on speaking Latin to his own detriment, and Sencer, the city wit who turns Sir Harry's ignorance to his own advantage, can be read as a self-conscious statement on Heywood's part. As the challenge between Sir Boniface and Sencer gets under way, the latter mentions that he was a student at Peterhouse, Cambridge, the college which Heywood attended before moving to London (for more details, see Glossarial Note 4.1.54). According to F. G. Fleay, Heywood acted Sencer himself. By drawing his audience's attention to these intriguing biographical links, the dramatist, who had made a living and built his reputation within the fast-growing, entrepreneurial world of the London public playhouses instead of pursuing an academic career, puts himself "on the map".

Sonia Massai

The Wise Woman of Hoxton

DRAMATIS PERSONAE

The Persons in the Play

YOUNG [ROBIN] CHARTLEY,
a wild-headed gentleman

BOYSTER,
a blunt fellow

SENCER,
a conceited gentleman

HARINGFIELD,
a civil gentleman

LUCE,
a goldsmith's daughter

LUCE'S FATHER,
a goldsmith

JOSEPH,
the goldsmith's apprentice

OLD MASTER CHARTLEY,
[*Chartley's father, a country gentleman*]

[SERVING-MAN 1]
Young Chartley's man

[GILES]
old Chartley's man

SIR HARRY,
a knight who is no piece of a scholar

GRATIANA,
Sir Harry's daughter

TABOR,
Sir Harry's man

SIR BONIFACE,
an ignorant pedant, or schoolmaster

The WISE WOMAN *of* HOXTON,
who bears the name of the drama

A COUNTRYMAN,
client to the Wise Woman

A KITCHEN MAID *and* TWO CITIZENS' WIVES, [*who*] *come to the Wise Woman for counsel*

[LUCE 2]
[*a young country gentlewoman*]

[SERVING-MAN 2]
[*Gratiana's man*]

ACT 1, SCENE 1

Enter, as newly come from play, four young gentlemen, Master CHARTLEY, *Master* SENCER, *Master* BOYSTER, *and Master* HARINGFIELD

Chartley Price of my life! Now if the devil have bones,
These dice are made of his. Was ever such a cast
Seen in this age? Could any gull in Europe,
Saving myself, fling such a cast?

Boyster Aye.

Chartley No.

Boyster Yes.

Chartley But I say no. I have lost
An hundred pound, and I will have my saying.

Boyster I have lost another hundred, I'll have mine.
Aye, yes, I flung a worse – a worse by odds.

Chartley I cry you mercy, sir, losers may speak.
I'll not except 'gainst you, but let me see –
Which of these two that pocket up our cash
Dares contradict me?

Sencer Sir, not I.
I say you have had bad casting.

Haringfield So say I.

Chartley I say this hat's not made of wool.
Which of you all dares say the contrary?

Sencer It may be 'tis a beaver.

Haringfield Very likely so. 'Tis not wool, but a plain beaver.

Chartley 'Tis wool, but which of you dares say so? [*Aside*] I would fain pick a quarrel with them, to get some of my money again; but the slaves, now they have got it, are too wise to part with it –
I say it is not black.

Haringfield So say we too.

Boyster 'Tis false! His cap's of wool; 'tis black, and wool,
And wool, and black.

Chartley I have nought to say to losers –
[*aside*] Have I nothing left to set at a cast?
Aye, finger, must you be set in gold,
And not a jot of silver in my purse? –
A bale of fresh dice! Ho, come at this ring!

Sencer Fie, Master Chartley. 'Tis time to give over.

Chartley That's the winner's phrase. Hold me play, or he that hath uncrowned me, I'll take a speedy order with him.

Boyster Fresh dice! This jewel I will venture more;
Take this and all. I'll play in spite of luck.

Haringfield Since you will needs, trip for the dice. I see it is hard to go a winner from this company.

Chartley The dice are mine. This diamond I value at twenty marks; I'll venture it at a throw.

Haringfield 'Tis set you.

Chartley Then, at all! [*Throws the dice*] All's mine. Nay, Master Boyster, I bar you: let us work upon the winners. Gramercy, *cinques*! Nay, though I owe you no quarrel, yet you must give me leave to draw.

Haringfield I had rather you should draw your sword,
Than draw my money thus.

Chartley Again, sweet dice!
Nay, I bar swearing. Gentlemen, let's play patiently. Well, this at the candlestick, so –

Boyster Now, dice, at all! [CHARTLEY *and* BOYSTER *throw*]
Todo, quoth the Spaniard.

Sencer Here's precious luck.

Boyster Why, *via*! [*throws again*] I think 'tis quicksilver:
It goes and comes so fast. There's life in this.

Haringfield He passes all with treys.

Chartley With treys, how say by that? Oh! He's old dog at bowls and treys.

Sencer Lend me some money. Be my half one cast.
I'll once out-brave this gamester with a throw.
So, now the dice are mine, will be my half?

Haringfield I will.

Sencer Then once I'll play the frank gamester.
Let me but see how much you both can make,
And I'll cast at all, all, every cross.

Chartley Now, bless us all! What, will you every cross?

Sencer I will not leave myself one cross to bless me.

Boyster I set.

Chartley And so do I.

Sencer Why then, at all! *Flings out*

How! –

Chartley Nay, swear not, let's play patiently.

Sencer Damn'd dice! Did ever gamester see the like?

Boyster Never, never.

Sencer Was ever known such casting?

Chartley Drunk nor sober, I never saw a man cast worse.

Sencer I'll prove this hat of mine a helmet.
Which of you here dares say the contrary?

Chartley As fair an helmet as any man in Europe needs to wear.

Sencer Chartley, thy hat is black.

Chartley Upon better recollection,
'Tis so indeed.

Sencer I say, 'tis made of wool.

Chartley True. My losing had took away my senses, both of seeing and feeling, but better luck hath brought them to their right temper.
But come, a pox of dice; 'tis time to give over.

Sencer All times are times for winners to give over,
But not for them that lose. I'll play till midnight,
But I will change my luck.

Haringfield Come, come, you shall not.
Give over. Tush, give over; do, I pray,
And choose the fortune of some other hour.
Let's not like debauch'd fellows, play our clothes,
Belts, rapiers, nor our needful ornaments.
'Tis childish, not becoming gentlemen.
Play was at first ordain'd to pass the time;

And, sir, you but abuse the use of play
To employ it otherwise.

Sencer You may persuade me. For once I'll leave a loser.

Chartley Then come, put on your helmet; let's leave this abominable game, and find out some better exercise. I cannot endure this chafing when men lose.

Sencer And there's not a more testy, waspish companion than thyself when thou art a loser, and yet thou must be vexing others with 'Play patiently, Gentlemen', and 'Let's have no swearing'.

Chartley A sign that I can give good counsel better than take it. But say, where be the prettiest wenches, my hearts?

Sencer Well remembered. This puts me in mind of an appointment I had with a gentlewoman of some respect.

Chartley I have you sir, I have you; but I think you will never have her. 'Tis Gratiana, the knight's daughter, in Gracious Street. Have I touched you?

Sencer You have come somewhat near me, but touched me not. Master Haringfield, will you bear me company thither? Have you seen the gentlewoman, Master Chartley?

Chartley Never, sir.

Sencer How have you heard of her?

Chartley That she hath … , as other women have;
That she goes for a maid, as others do.

Sencer I can assure you, she is a proper gentlewoman.

Chartley Then if she have you, she is like to have a proper gentleman.

Sencer You should tell them so that know it not. Adieu, gentlemen. *Exeunt* SENCER *and* HARINGFIELD

Boyster I am glad yet they go so lightly away.

Chartley What will you do, Master Boyster?

Boyster Somewhat.

Chartley You will not acquaint me with your business?

Boyster No. [*Aside*] I am in love, my head is full of proclamations. There is a thing called a virgin; nature hath showed her art in making her. Court her I cannot, but I'll do as I may.

Chartley Do you go or stay, sir?

Boyster Go.

Chartley You before; I'll follow. [*Exit* BOYSTER]
He thinks with his blunt humour to enter as far as I with my sharp. No, my true Trojan, no. There is a fair, sweet, modest rogue, her name is Luce. With this dandiprat, this pretty little ape's face, is yon blunt fellow in love; and no marvel, for she hath a brow bewitching, eyes ravishing, and a tongue enchanting. And indeed she hath no fault in the world but one, and that is, she is honest. And were it not for that, she were the only sweet rogue in Christendom. As I live, I love her extremely, and to enjoy her would give anything. But the fool stands in her own light, and will do nothing without marriage. But what should I do

marrying? I can better endure gyves, than bands of matrimony. But, in this meditation, I am glad I have won my money again. Nay, and she may be glad of it too: for the girl is but poor, and in my pocket I have laid up a stock for her, 'tis put to use already. And if I meet not with a dice-house or an ordinary by the way, no question but I may increase it to a sum. Well, I'll unto the Exchange to buy her some pretty novelty. That done, I'll visit my little rascal and solicit instantly. [*Exit*]

ACT 1, SCENE 2

Enter LUCE *in a sempster's shop, at work upon a laced handkerchief, and* JOSEPH, *an apprentice*

Luce Where is my father, Joseph?

Joseph Mistress, above,
And prays you to attend below a little.

Luce I do not love to sit thus publicly;
And yet upon the traffic of our wares,
Our provident eyes and presence must still wait.
Do you attend the shop, I'll ply my work.
I see my father is not jealous of me,
That trusts me to the open view of all.
The reason is, he knows my thoughts are chaste,
And my care such as that it needs the awe
Of no strict overseer.

Enter Master BOYSTER

Boyster Yonder's Luce. – Save thee.

Luce And you too, sir. You're welcome; want you ought,
I pray, in which our trade may furnish you?

Boyster Yes.

Luce Joseph, show the gentleman –

Boyster 'Tis here that I would buy.

Luce What do you mean, sir? Speak, what is't you lack?
I pray you, wherefore do you fix your eyes
So firmly in my face? What would you have?

Boyster Thee.

Luce Me?

Boyster Yes, thee.

Luce Your pleasure is to jest, and so I take it.
Pray give me leave, sir, to intend my work.

Boyster You are fair.

Luce You flout me.

Boyster You are, go to, you are,
I'd vex him that should say the contrary.

Luce Well, you may say your pleasure.

Boyster I love thee.

Luce Oh! Sir!

Boyster As I live, I do.

Luce Now, as I am a true maid,
The most religious oath that I dare swear,
I hold myself indebted to your love,

And I am sorry there remains in me
No power how to requite it.

Boyster Love me, prethee now; do, if thou canst.

Luce I cannot.

Boyster Prethee, if thou canst.

Luce Indeed, I cannot.

Boyster Yet ask thine heart, and see what may be done.

Luce In troth I am sorry you should spend a sigh
For my sake unrequited, or a tear,
Aye, or a word.

Boyster 'Tis no matter for my words; they are not many,
And those not very wise ones neither.

Luce Yet I beseech you, spend no more in vain.
I scorn you not; disdain's as far from me
As are the two poles distant. Therefore, sir,
Because I would not hold you in suspense,
But tell you what at first to trust unto,
Thus in a word, I must not fancy you.

Boyster Must not?

Luce I cannot, nor I may not.

Boyster I am gone:
Thou hast given me, Luce, a bone to gnaw upon. *Exit*

Luce Alas, that beauty should be sought of more
Than can enjoy it. Might I have my wish,
I would seem fair but only in his eye
That should possess me in a nuptial tie.

Enter young Master CHARTLEY *with gloves, ring, purse, etc.*

Chartley Morrow, Luce. In exchange of this kiss, [*kisses her*] see what I have brought thee from the Exchange.

Luce What mean you, sir, by this?

Chartley Guess that by the circumstance: here's a ring, wear't for my sake; twenty angels, pocket them, you fool. Come, come, I know thou art a maid; say nay, and take them.

Luce
Sweet Master Chartley, do not fasten on me
More than with ease I can shake off. Your gift
I reverence, yet refuse. And, I pray tell me,
Why do you make so many errands hither?
Send me so many letters? Fasten on me
So many favours? What's your meaning in't?

Chartley Hark in thine ear, I'll tell thee. [LUCE *walks off*] Nay, hear me out. [*Aside*] Is't possible so soft a body should have so hard a soul? – [*To* LUCE] Nay, now I know my penance: you will be angry, and school me for tempting your modesty. [*aside*] A fig for this modesty; it hinders many a good man from many a good turn, and that's all the good it doth. – If thou but knew'st, Luce, how I love thee, thou would'st be far more tractable. Nay, I bar chiding when you speak. I'll stop thy lips if thou dost but offer an angry word, by this hand I'll do't, and with this hand too. Go to, now; what say you?

Luce
Sir, if you love me, as you say you do,
Show me the fruits thereof.

Chartley The stock I can, thou may'st see the fruits hereafter.

Luce Can I believe you love me, when you seek
The shipwreck of mine honour?

Chartley Honour! There's another word to flap in a man's mouth. Honour! What, should'st thou and I stand upon our honour, that were neither of us yet right worshipful?

Luce I am sorry, sir, I have lent so large an ear
To such a bad discourse; and I protest
After this hour, never to do the like.
I must confess, of all the gentlemen
That ever courted me, you have possessed
The best part in my thoughts. But this coarse language
Exiles you quite from thence. Sir, had you come,
Instead of changing this mine honest name
Into a strumpet's, to have honoured me
With the chaste title of a modest wife,
I had reserv'd an ear for all your suits.
But since I see your rudeness finds no limit,
I leave you to your lust.

Chartley You shall not, Luce.

Luce Then keep your tongue within more moderate bounds.

Chartley I will, as I am virtuous, I will.
[*Aside*] I told you the second word would be marriage. It makes a man forfeit his freedom, and makes him walk ever after with a chain at his heels, or a jackanapes hanging at his elbow. Marriage is like *Dædalus*'s labyrinth, and being once in, there's no finding the way out. Well, I love this little property most intolerably, and I must set her on the last, though it cost me all the shoes in my shop. –

Well, Luce, thou seest my stomach is come down.
Thou hast my heart already; there's my hand.

Luce But in what way?

Chartley Nay, I know not the way yet, but I hope to find it hereafter by your good direction.

Luce I mean, in what manner? In what way?

Chartley In the way of marriage, in the way of honesty, in the way that was never gone yet. I hope thou art a maid, Luce?

Luce Yes, sir; and I accept it. In exchange
Of this your hand, you shall receive my heart.

Chartley A bargain, an there's earnest on thy lips. [*Kisses her*]

Luce I'll call my father, sir, to witness it.
See, here he comes.

Enter [LUCE'S FATHER], *a plain citizen*

Chartley Father, save you. You have happened on an untoward son-in-law. Here I am; how do you like me?

Luce's father Sir, I was nearer than you were aware,
And overheard both sum and circumstance.

Chartley [*aside*] Then I perceive you are an old eavesdropper – But what do you think of it, father?

Luce's father I entertain the motion with all love,
And I rejoice my daughter is preferr'd
And rais'd to such a match. I heard the contract,
And will confirm it gladly. But pray, sir,

When shall the merry day be?

Chartley Marry, even tomorrow, by that we can see. Nay, we'll lose no more time. I'll take order for that.

Luce Stay but a month.

Chartley A month! Thou can'st not hire me to't. Why Luce, if thou be'st hungry, can'st thou stay a month from meat? Nay, if I see my diet before me, I love to fall to when I have a stomach. Here [*gives her money*]; buy thee a new smock. Let's have a new bed too, and look it be strong. [*Gives her a box*] There's a box of rings and jewels, lay them up. [*to* LUCE'S FATHER] Ah, sirrah, methinks the very name of wedlock hath brought me to a night-cap already, and I am grown civil on the sudden. – [*Gives* LUCE *more money*] There's more money for dishes, platters, ladles, candlesticks, etc., as I shall find them set down in the inventory.

Luce's father But whom shall we invite unto the wedding?

Enter LUCE 2, *a young country gentlewoman, in the habit of a page, and overhears their discourse*

Chartley Aye, thereby hangs a tale. We will have no more at our marriage but myself, to say, 'I take thee, Luce', thou to say, 'I, Luce, take thee, Robin', the vicar to put us together, and you, father, to play the clerk and cry 'Amen'.

Luce's father Your reason for that?

Chartley I would not for a world it should be known to my friends, or come to my father's ear. It may be ten thousand pounds out of my way for the present. Therefore, this is my conceit: let us be married privately, and Luce shall live like a maid still and bear the name. 'Tis nothing, Luce; it is a common thing in this age to go for a maid and be none. I'll frequent the house secretly. Fear not girl, though I revel abroad a-days, I'll be with thee to bring a-nights, my little whiting-mop.

Luce But so I may incur a public scandal,
By your so oft frequenting to my chamber.

Chartley Scandal? What scandal? Why, to stop the mouth of all scandal, after some few days, do I appear in my likeness, married man and honest housekeeper, and then what becomes of your scandal? Come, send for Master Vicar, and what we do, let's do suddenly.

Luce 2 [*aside*] Cold comfort for me.

Luce If you purpose to be so privately married,
I know one excellent at such an exploit.
Are you not acquainted with the Wise Woman of Hoxton?

Chartley Oh, the witch, the beldam, the hag of Hoxton.

Luce The same; but I hold her to be of no such condition. I will anon make a step thither, and punctually acquaint her with all our proceedings. She is never without a Sir John at her elbow, ready for such a stratagem.

Chartley Well, be it so then. *Exeunt* [*all but* LUCE 2]

Luce 2 Heigh-ho! Have I disguised myself, and stolen out of the country thus far, and can light of no better news to entertain me? Oh, this wild-headed, wicked Chartley, whom nothing will tame! To this gallant was I, poor gentlewoman, betrothed and the marriage day appointed. But he, out of a fantastic and giddy humour, before the time prefixed, posts up to London. After him come I thus habited, and you see my welcome, to be an ear-witness of his second contracting. Modesty would not suffer me to discover myself; otherwise, I should have gone near to have marred the match. I heard them talk of Hoxton and a wise woman, where these aims shall be brought to action. I'll see if I can insinuate myself into her service. That's my next project; and now, good luck of my side. *Exit*

ACT 2, SCENE 1

Enter the WISE WOMAN *and her clients: a* COUNTRYMAN *with a urinal, four women like citizens' wives,* TABOR *a serving-man, and a* KITCHEN MAID

Wise Woman [*to herself*] Fie, fie! What a toil and a moil it is,
For a woman to be wiser than all her neighbours –
I pray, good people, press not too fast upon me; though I have two ears, I can hear but one at once. [*to the* COUNTRYMAN]
You with the urine.

Enter LUCE 2 *and stands aside,* [*unseen*]

Countryman Here, forsooth, mistress.

Wise Woman And who distilled this water?

Countryman My wife's limbeck, if it please you.

Wise Woman And where doth the pain hold her most?

Countryman Marry, at her heart, forsooth.

Wise Woman Aye, at her heart. She hath a griping at her heart?

Countryman You have hit it right.

Wise Woman Nay, I can see so much in the urine.

Luce 2 [*aside*] Just so much as is told her.

Wise Woman She hath no pain in her head, hath she?

Countryman No, indeed; I never heard her complain of her

hcad.

Wise Woman I told you so. Her pain lies all at her heart.
Alas, good heart! But how feels she her stomach?

Countryman Oh, queasy and sick at stomach.

Wise Woman Aye, I warrant you. I think I can see as far into a millstone as another. You have heard of Mother Nottingham, who, for her time, was prettily well skilled in casting of waters. And after her, Mother Bomby. And then there is one Hatfield in Pepper Alley; he doth pretty well for a thing that's lost. There's another in Coldharbour that's skilled in the planets. Mother Sturton in Golden Lane is for forespeaking. Mother Philips of the Bankside for the weakness of the back. And then there's a very reverend matron on Clerkenwell Green, good at many things. Mistress Mary on the Bankside is for 'recting a figure. And one – what do you call her – in Westminster, that practises the book and the key, and the sieve and the shears. And all do well, according to their talent. For myself, let the world speak. Hark you, my friend, you shall take – *Whispers*

Luce 2 [*aside*] 'Tis strange the ignorant should be thus fool'd.
What can this witch, this wizard, or old trot,
Do by enchantment or by magic spell?
Such as profess that art should be deep scholars.
What reading can this simple woman have?
'Tis palpable gross foolery. [*Exit* COUNTRYMAN]

Wise Woman Now, friend, your business?

Tabor I have stolen out of my master's house, forsooth,

with the kitchen maid, and I am come to know of you, whether it be my fortune to have her or no.

Wise Woman And what's your suit, Lady?

Kitchen Maid Forsooth, I come to know whether I be a maid or no.

Wise Woman Why, art thou in doubt of that?

Kitchen Maid It may be I have more reason than all the world knows.

Tabor Nay, if thou com'st to know whether thou be'st a maid or no, I had best ask to know whether I be with child or no.

Wise Woman Withdraw into the parlour there; I'll but talk with this other gentlewoman, and I'll resolve you presently.

Tabor Come, Cicely, if she cannot resolve thee, I can; and, in the case of a maidenhead, do more than she, I warrant thee.

Exeunt [TABOR *and* KITCHEN MAID

Citizen's Wife Forsooth, I am bold, as they say.

Wise Woman You are welcome, gentlewoman –

Citizen's Wife I would not have it known to my neighbours, that I come to a wise woman for anything, by my truly.

Wise Woman For should your husband come and find you here –

Citizen's Wife My husband? Woman, I am a widow!

Wise Woman Where are my brains? 'Tis true, you are a widow, and you dwell – let me see – I can never remember that place –

Citizen's Wife In Kent Street.

Wise Woman Kent Street, Kent Street! And I can tell you wherefore you come.

Citizen's Wife Why, and say true?

Wise Woman You are a wag; you are a wag. Why, what do you think now I would say?

Citizen's Wife Perhaps, to know how many husbands I should have?

Wise Woman And if I should say so, should I say amiss?

Citizen's Wife I think you are a witch.

Wise Woman In, in. I'll but read a little of *Ptolemy* and *Erra Pater*. And, when I have cast a figure, I'll come to you presently. [*Exeunt* CITIZENS' WIVES] Now, wag, what wouldst thou have?

Luce 2 [*aside*] If this were a wise woman, she could tell that without asking. Now, methinks, I should come to know whether I were a boy or a girl. – Forsooth, I lack a service.

Wise Woman By my fidelity, and I want a good trusty lad.

Luce 2 [*aside*] Now could I sigh and say, "Alas, this is some bawd trade-fallen, and, out of her wicked experience, is come to be reputed wise". I'll serve her, be't but to pry into the mystery of her science.

Wise Woman [*aside*] A proper stripling, and a wise, I warrant him. – Here's a penny for thee. I'll hire thee for a year by the Statute of Winchester. Prove true and honest, and thou shalt want nothing that a good boy –

Luce 2 [*aside*] Here, Wise Woman, you are out again: I shall want what a good boy should have, whilst I live. Well, here I shall live both unknown and my sex unsuspected – But whom have we here?

Enter Master HARINGFIELD *and* CHARTLEY, *half drunk*

Chartley Come, Haringfield; now we have been drinking of Mother Redcap's ale, let us now go make some sport with the Wise Woman.

Haringfield We shall be thought very wise men, of all such as shall see us go in to the Wise Woman's.

Chartley See, here she is. How now, witch? How now, hag? How now, beldam? You are the Wise Woman, are you? And have wit to keep yourself warm enough, I warrant you.

Wise Woman Out, thou knave.

Luce 2 [*aside*] And will these wild oats never be sown?

Chartley You enchantress, sorceress, she-devil; you Madam Hecate, Lady Proserpine. You are too old, you hag, now, for conjuring up spirits yourself; but you keep pretty young witches under your roof that can do that.

Wise Woman I, or my family, conjure up any spirits? I defy thee, thou young hare-brained –

Haringfield Forbear him till he have his senses about him, and I shall then hold thee for a wise woman indeed. Otherwise, I shall doubt thou hast thy name for nothing. – Come friend, away, if thou lovest me.

Chartley Away, you old dromedary! I'll come one of these nights, and make a racket amongst your she-caterwaulers.

Haringfield I prethee, let's be civil.

Chartley Out of my sight, thou she-mastiff!

Exeunt [CHARTLEY *and* HARINGFIELD]

Luce 2 Patience, sweet mistress.

Wise Woman Now bless me, he hath put me into such a fear as makes all my bones to dance and rattle in my skin. I'll be revenged on that swaggering companion.

Luce 2 Mistress, I wish you would. He's a mere madcap, and all his delight is in misusing such reverend matrons as yourself.

Wise Woman Well, what's thy name, boy?

Luce 2 I am even little better than a turnbroach, for my name is Jack.

Wise Woman Honest Jack, if thou could'st but devise how I might cry quittance with this cutting Dick, I will go near to adopt thee my son and heir.

Luce 2 Mistress, there is a way, and this it is:
Tomorrow morning doth this gentleman
Intend to marry with one Mistress Luce,
A goldsmith's daughter. Do you know the maid?

Wise Woman My daughter, and a pretty smug-fac'd girl.
I had a note but late from her, and she means to be with me in th'evening; for I have bespoke Sir Boniface to marry her in the morning.

Luce 2 Do but prevent this gallant of his wife,

And then your wrongs shall be reveng'd at full.

Wise Woman I'll do't, as I am matron; aye, and show him a new trick for his learning.

Enter Master BOYSTER

Boyster Morrow.

Wise Woman You're welcome, sir.

Boyster Art wise?

Luce 2 [*aside*] He should be wise, because he speaks few words.

Wise Woman I am as I am, and there's an end.

Boyster Can'st conjure?

Wise Woman Oh! That's a foul word! But I can tell you your fortune, as they say. I have some little skill in palmistry, but never had to do with the devil.

Boyster And had the devil never anything to do with thee? Thou look'st somewhat like his dam. Look on me, can'st tell what I ail?

Wise Woman Can you tell yourself? I should guess you be mad, or not well in your wits.

Boyster Th'art wise, I am so. Men being in love are mad, and I being in love, am so.

Wise Woman Nay, if I see your complexion once, I think I can guess as near as another.

Boyster One Mistress Luce I love. Know'st thou her, grannam?

Wise Woman As well as the beggar knows his dish. Why, she is one of my daughters.

Boyster Make her my wife, I'll give thee forty pieces.

Luce 2 [*to the* WISE WOMAN] Take them, mistress, to be revenged on Chartley.

Wise Woman A bargain, strike me luck! Cease all your sorrow,
Fair Luce shall be your bride betimes tomorrow.

Boyster Th'art a good grannam; and, but that thy teeth stand like hedge-stakes in thy head, I'd kiss thee.

Exit [BOYSTER]

Wise Woman Pray, will you in? Come hither, Jack, I have
A new trick come into my head. Wilt thou
Assist me in't?

Luce 2 If it concern the crossing of the marriage with Mistress Luce, I'll do't, whatever it be.

Wise Woman Thou shalt be 'tired like a woman. Can you make a courtesy, take small strides, simper, and seem modest? => is returning to her real identity
Methinks thou hast a woman's voice already.

Luce 2 Doubt not of me; I'll act them naturally.

Wise Woman I have conceited to have Luce married to this blunt gentleman, she mistaking him for Chartley; and Chartley shall marry thee, being a boy, and take thee for Luce. Wilt not be excellent?

Luce 2 Oh! Super, super-excellent!

Wise Woman Play but thy part, as I'll act mine. I'll fit him with a wife, I warrant him.

Luce 2 And a wife I'll warrant him. *Exeunt*

ACT 2, SCENE 2

Enter old SIR HARRY *and his man* TABOR

Sir Harry Ha! Then thou sawest them whispering with my daughter?

Tabor I saw them, if it shall please you, not whisper, but –

Sir Harry How then, thou knave?

Tabor Marry, sir knight, I saw them in sad talk; but to say they were directly whispering, I am not able.

Sir Harry Why, Tabor, that sad talk was whispering.

Tabor Nay, they did not greatly whisper, for I heard what was said; and what was said, I have the wit to keep to myself.

Sir Harry What said the unthrift, Tabor? Tell me, knave!
Tell me, good knave, what did the unthrift say?

Tabor I am loath to be called in question about men and women's matters, but as soon as ever he saw your daughter, I heard what was spoken.

Sir Harry Here, sirrah, take thy quarter's wages aforehand, and tell me all their words, and what their greeting was at their first encounter. Hold thine hand.

[*Gives* TABOR *money*

Tabor Thanks, noble sir, and now I'll tell you. Your daughter being walking to take the air of the fields, and I before her, whom should we meet just in the nick?

Sir Harry Just in the nick, man?

Tabor In the highway, I meant, sir.

Sir Harry Ha! And what conference passed between them, Tabor?

Tabor As well as my pipe can utter, you shall know, sir. This gentleman meeting with my young mistress full butt – imagine you were she, and I young Master Sencer – now, there you come, and here I meet you. He comes in this manner, and put off his hat in this fashion.

Sir Harry Aye, but what said he?

Tabor "Be with you, fair gentlewoman". And so goes quite away, and scarce so much as once looked back. And if this were language to offer to a young lady, judge you.

Sir Harry But spoke he nothing else?

Tabor Nothing, as I am true.

Sir Harry Why man, all this was nothing.

Tabor Yes, sir; it was as much as my quarter's wages aforehand.

Enter Master SENCER, *Master* HARINGFIELD *and* GRATIANA

Gratiana [*aside*] Here are two gentlemen with great desire
Crave conference with my father. Here he is –
Now, gallants, you may freely speak your minds.

Sencer Save you, sir, my name is Sencer; I am a Northamptonshire gentleman, born to a thousand pound land by the year. I love your daughter, and I am come to crave your good will.

Sir Harry Have you my daughter's, that you covet mine?

Sencer No, sir, but I hope in time I shall have.

Sir Harry So hope not I, sir. Sir, my daughter's young, and you a gentleman unknown. Sencer? Ah, Sencer! Oh, sir, your name I now remember well: 'tis ranked 'mongst unthrifts, dicers, swaggerers, and drunkards. Were not you brought before me, some month since, for beating of the watch? By the same token, I sent you to the counter.

Sencer I confess myself to have been in that action, but note the cause, Sir. You could not have pleasured me so much, in giving me a piece of gold, as at the same time to help me to that counter.

Sir Harry Why, sir, what cause had you to beat the watch
And raise a midnight tumult in the streets?

Sencer Nay, but hear me, sweet Sir Harry. Being somewhat late at supper at the Mitre, the doors were shut at my lodging. I knocked at three or four places more, all were abed and fast. Inns, taverns, none would give me entertainment. Now, would you have had me despaired and lain in the streets? No, I bethought me of a trick worth two of that, and presently devised, having at that time a charge of money about me, to be lodged, and safely too.

Sir Harry As how, I pray you?

Sencer Marry, thus. I had knocked my heels against the ground a good while, knew not where to have a bed for love nor money. Now what did I, but spying the watch, went and hit the constable a good souse on the ear, who provided me of a lodging presently. And the next day, being brought before your worship, I was then sent thither back again, where I lay three or four days without control.

Sir Harry Oh, you're a gallant! Is that gentleman a suitor too?

Haringfield I am a suitor in my friend's behalf,
No otherwise, I can assure you, sir.
He is a gentleman descended well,
Derived from a good house, well qualified,
And well possessed; but that which most should move you,
He loves your daughter.

Gratiana [*aside*] But were I to choose,
Which of these two should please my fancy best,
I sooner should affect this gentleman
For his mild carriage and his fair discourse
Than my hot suitor. Ruffians I detest;
A smooth and square behaviour likes me best.

Sencer What say you to me, lady?

Gratiana You had best ask my father what I should say.

Sencer Are you angry, sweet lady, that I asked your father's consent?

Gratiana No; if you can get his consent to marry him, shall it displease me?

Haringfield Indeed you therein much forget yourself,
To sound her father ere you tasted her.
You should have first sought means for her good-will,

And after compassed his.

Sir Harry He can prevail with neither. Gentlemen,
If you will come to revel, you are welcome;
If to my table, welcome; if to use me
In any grateful office, welcome too.
But if you come as suitors, there's the door.

Sencer The door?

Sir Harry I say the door.

Sencer Why, sir? Tell not me of your door, nor going out of it. Your company is fair and good, and so is your daughter's. I'll stay here this twelve-month, ere I'll offer to trouble your door.

Sir Harry Sir, but you shall not. Tabor! Where's that knave?

Sencer Why, sir, I hope you do not mean to make us dance, that you call for a tabor.

Haringfield [*to* SENCER] Nay, Master Sencer, do not urge the knight.
He is incensed now; choose a fitter hour,
And tempt his love in that. Old men are testy:
Their rage, if stood against, grows violent,
But suffered and forborn, confounds itself.

Sir Harry Where's Tabor?

Tabor [*coming forward*] At hand, noble master.

Sir Harry Show them the door.

Tabor That I will, and take money too, if it please them.

Sencer Is thy name Tabor?

Tabor I am so yclept, sir.

Sencer And, Tabor, are you appointed to give us Jack

Drum's Entertainment?

Tabor Why, sir, you do not play upon me?

Sencer Though I cannot, yet I have known an hare that could. But knight, thou doest not forbid us thine house?

Sir Harry Yes, and forewarn it too.

Sencer But, by thy favour, we may choose whether we will take any warning or no. Well, farewell old knight. Though thou forbidst me thine house, I'll honour thee and extol thee. And though thou keepst me from thy daughter, thou shalt not hinder me to love her and admire her and, by thy favour, sometimes to see her. A cat may look at a king, and so may I at her. Give me thine hand, knight; the next time I come into thy company, thou shalt not only bid me welcome, but hire me to stay with thee and thy daughter.

Sir Harry When I do that, enjoy my full consent
To marry Gratiana.

Sencer 'Tis a match,
Strike me luck. Wife that may be, farewell;
Father-in-law that must be, adieu.
Tabor, play before, my friend and I will dance after.

Sir Harry When I receive thee gladly to mine house
And wage thy stay, thou shalt have Gratiana;
Doubt not, thou shalt.

Exeunt [SENCER *and* HARINGFIELD *led by* TABOR]

Here's a strange humourist,
To come a-wooing. [*Re-enter* TABOR] Tabor, are they gone?

Tabor I have played them away, if it please your worship.

And yonder at the door attends a schoolmaster; you sent for him, if you remember, to teach my little young master and mistress.

Sir Harry A proper scholar. Pray him to come near.

Enter SIR BONIFACE, *a pedantical schoolmaster*

Sir Boniface *Eques honoratus; ave salutatus. Non video quid est in tergo, sed salve bona virgo.*

Sir Harry Sir, you may call me nicknames. If you love me, speak in your mother tongue, or, at the least, if learning be so much allied unto you that Latin unawares flows from your lips, to make your mind familiar with my knowledge, pray, utter it in English. What's your name?

Sir Boniface *Sit faustum tibi omen*;
I'll tell you my *nomen*.

Sir Harry Will you tell it to no men?
I'll entertain none ere I know their names.
Nay, if you be so dainty of your name,
You are not for my service.

Sir Boniface *Intende, vir nobilis.*

Sir Harry Not for twenty nobles:
Trust me, I will not buy your name so dear.

Sir Boniface [*aside*] O *ignorantia*! What it is to deal with stupidity? –
Sir Henry, Sir Henry; hear me one word:
I see, *preceptor legit, vos verum negligitis*.

Tabor I think he says we are a company of fools and nidgets, but I hope you shall not find us such, master schoolmaster.

Sir Harry Friend, friend; to cut off all vain circumstance,
Tell me your name, and answer me directly,
Plainly, and to my understanding too,
Or I shall leave you. Here's a deal of gibberish!

Sir Boniface *Vir bone.*

Sir Harry Nay, nay; make me no bones, but do't.

Sir Boniface Then, in plain vulgar English, I am called,
Sir Boniface Absee.

Sir Harry Why, this is somewhat like, Sir Boniface.
Give me thine hand. Thou art a proper man,
And in my judgement a great scholar too.
What shall I give thee by the year?

Sir Boniface I'll trust, sir, to your generosity.
I will not bargain, but account myself
Mille et mille modis bound to you.

Sir Harry I cannot leave my mills; they're farm'd already.
The stipend that I give shall be in money.

Tabor Sure, sir, this is some miller that comes to undermine you in the shape of a schoolmaster.

Gratiana You both mistake the scholar.

Sir Harry I understand my English, that I know;
What's more than modern doth surpass my reach.
Sir Boniface, come to me two days hence;
You shall receive an answer. I have now
Matters of some import that trouble me;
Thou shouldst be else dispatched.

Tabor Sir Boniface, if you come to live in our house,

and be a Familist amongst us, I shall desire your better acquaintance. Your name and my physiognomy should have some consanguinity, good Sir Boniface.

Sir Boniface *Quomodo vales, quomodo vales.*

Tabor Go with you to the alehouse? I like the motion well. I'll make an excuse out of doors and follow you. I am glad that we shall have a good fellow come into the house amongst us.

Sir Boniface *Vale vir magno.*

Sir Harry You shall not have me at Saint Magnus; my house is here in Gracious Street.

Sir Boniface I know it, sweet knight, I know it. Then *virgo formosa et domine gratiose valete.*

Sir Harry Aye, in Gracious Street you shall hear of me,
Sir Boniface. [*Exit* SIR BONIFACE]
He shall instruct my children, and to thee,
Fair Gratiana, read the Latin tongue.

Tabor Who shall? Sir Bawdy-face?

Sir Harry Sir Boniface, you fool.

Tabor His name is so hard to hit on.

Sir Harry Come, daughter, if things fall out as I intend,
My thoughts shall peace have, and these troubles end.

Exeun

ACT 3, SCENE 1

Enter LUCE 2 [*disguised as* JACK] *and the* WISE WOMAN

Wise Woman Jack, thou art my boy.

Luce 2 Mistress.

Wise Woman I'll be a mother to thee, no mistress. Come, lad, I must have thee sworn to the orders of my house and the secrets thereof.

Luce 2 As I am an honest lad, I am yours to command. But mistress, what mean all these women's pictures hanged here in your withdrawing-room?

Wise Woman I'll tell thee, boy. Marry, thou must be secret. When any citizens or young gentlemen come hither under a colour to know their fortunes, they look upon these pictures, and which of them they best like, she is ready with a wet finger. Here they have all the furniture belonging to a private chamber: bed, bed-fellow and all. But, mum! Thou knowest my meaning, Jack.

Luce 2 But I see, coming and going, maids, or such as go for maids, some of them as if they were ready to lie down, sometimes two or three delivered in one night. Then suddenly leave their brats behind them and convey themselves into the city again. What becomes of their children?

Wise Woman Those be kitchen maids and chambermaids, and sometimes good men's daughters, who having catched a clap and growing near their time, get leave to see their friends in the country for a week or so. Then hither they come, and for a matter of money here they are delivered. I have a midwife or two belonging to the house, and one Sir Boniface, a deacon, that makes a shift to christen the infants. We have poor, honest and secret neighbours that stand for common gossips. But dost not thou know this?

Luce 2 Yes, now I do. But what after becomes of the poor infants?

Wise Woman Why, in the night we send them abroad, and lay one at this man's door, and another at that, such as are able to keep them. And what after becomes of them, we enquire not. And this is another string to my bow.

Luce 2 [*aside*] Most strange, that woman's brain should apprehend
Such lawless, indirect and horrid means
For covetous gain! How many unknown trades
Women and men are free of, which they never
Had charter for? –
But, mistress, are you so cunning as you make yourself? You can neither write nor read; what do you with those books you so often turn over?

Wise Woman Why, tell the leaves. For to be ignorant, and seem ignorant, what greater folly?

Luce 2 [*aside*] Believe me, this is a cunning woman. Neither hath she her name for nothing, who out of her ignorance can fool so many that think themselves wise. – But wherefore have you built this little closet close to the door, where, sitting, you may hear every word spoken by all such as ask for you?

Wise Woman True, and therefore I built it. If any knock, you must to the door and question them, to find what they come about, if to this purpose, or to that. Now, they ignorantly telling thee their errand, which I sitting in my closet overhear, presently come forth and tell them the cause of their coming, with every word that hath passed between you in private, which, they admiring and thinking it to be miraculous, by their report I become thus famous.

Luce 2 This is no trade, but a mystery. And were I a wise woman, as indeed I am but a foolish boy, I need not live by your service. But mistress, we lose ourselves in this discourse. Is not this the morning in which I should be married?

Wise Woman Now, how had I forgot myself! Mistress Luce promised to be with me half an hour ago, but masked and disguised, and so shalt thou be too. Here's a black veil to hide thy face against the rest come. [LUCE 2 *puts on the veil*]

Enter SIR BONIFACE

Sir Boniface *Sit tibi bona dies, salus et quies.*

Wise Woman Into the withdrawing-room, Sir Boniface.

Sir Boniface Without any compunction,
I will make the conjunction.

Wise Woman Now keep thy countenance, boy. *Exit*

Luce 2 Fear not me. I have as good a face in a mask as any lady in the land could wish to have. – [*Aside*] But, to my heart, he comes or he comes not. Now am I in a pitiful perplexity, until I see the event of all.

Wise Woman No more Jack now, but Mistress Luce.

Luce 2 I warrant you, mistress. – [*Aside*] That it happens so luckily, that my name should be Luce too, to make the marriage more firm!

Enter CHARTLEY *disguised and in a vizard*

Chartley My honey-sweet hag, where's Luce?

Wise Woman Here, sweetheart, but disguised and veiled, as you are vizarded.

Chartley But what's the reason we are thus hoodwinked?

Wise Woman No discovery of yourselves for a million! There's Sir Boniface within; shall he blab who you are? Besides, there's a young heir that hath stolen a lord's daughter from the court, and would not have their faces seen for a world. Cannot you be content to fare well and keep your own counsel? And see, yonder they come.

Enter [*severally*] BOYSTER *in a vizard and* LUCE *masked*

Chartley Gramercy, my sugar-candy sweet trot.

Wise Woman Mum, no more words.

Chartley If the great heir and the young lady be so dainty of their complexions, they shall see – my sweet Luce –

we can vizard it with the best of them.

[CHARTLEY *and* LUCE 2 *stand aside*]

Luce [*looking at* BOYSTER, *aside*] That gentleman, by the Wise Woman's description, should be Master Chartley.

Boyster [*looking at* LUCE, *aside*] That gallant wench, if my grannam fable not, should be Luce. [*To the* WISE WOMAN] But what be those other?

Wise Woman You wrong me but to ask; who but a young heir and a lady of the court. That's Luce, take her, and keep your promise.

Boyster *Pocas palabras.* [*Stands aside*]

Wise Woman [*to* LUCE] That's Chartley, take him Luce.

Luce But who be they?

Wise Woman A lord and lady shall Sir Boniface stay –
Rather then so, strive who should lead the way.

Exeunt CHARTLEY *with* [LUCE 2]*, and* BOYSTER *with* LUCE

Now Jack, my boy, keep thine own counsel and countenance, and I shall cry quittance with my young gallant. Well, by this time Sir Boniface is at his book. But because there is a mistake, known only to my boy and myself, the marriage shall be no sooner ended but I'll disturb them by some sudden outcry, and that too before they have leisure to unmask and make known themselves one to another. For if the deceit were known, I should fall into the danger of that young mad rascal. And now this double apprehension of the lord and the lady shall fetch me off from all. I know it is Sir Boniface's custom to make short work, and hath dispatched by this. And now, Wise Woman, try if thou canst bestir thyself like to a madwoman – [*she shouts*] Shift for yourselves, warrants and pursuivants! Away! Warrants and pursuivants! Shift for yourselves.

Re-enter CHARTLEY, [LUCE 2], BOYSTER, [LUCE] *and* SIR BONIFACE, *affrighted and amazed*

Chartley I'll take this way.

Boyster I this. *Exeunt* [CHARTLEY *and* BOYSTER]

Sir Boniface *Curro, curris, cucurri,*
My cheeks are all murrey,
And I am gone in a hurry. *Exit*

Luce O heaven! What shall become of me?

Luce 2 [*aside*] I know what shall become of me already.

Wise Woman Oh, sweet daughter, shift clothes with this lady! Nay, as thou lov'st thy credit and mine, change habits. So, if thou be'st taken in her garments, finding the mistake, they will let thee pass; and should they meet her in thine, not knowing her, would no way question her. And this prove to both your securities and my safety.

Luce As fast as I can, good mother. [*They exchange clothes*] So Madam, farewell. [*Exit*]

Luce 2 All happy joys betide you. *Exit*

Wise Woman Ha, ha! Let me hold my sides and laugh. Here were even a plot to make a play on, but that Chartley is so fooled by my boy Jack. Well, he'll make a notable wag, I'll warrant him. All the jest

will be, if Boyster should meet with him in Luce's habit, which he hath now on, he would think himself merely gulled and cheated. And should Chartley meet with Luce as she is now robed, he would be confident he had married her. Let me see how many trades have I to live by: first, I am a wise woman and a fortune-teller, and under that I deal in physic and forespeaking, in palmistry, and recovering of things lost. Next, I undertake to cure mad folks. Then I keep gentlewomen lodgers to furnish such chambers as I let out by the night. Then I am provided for bringing young wenches to bed. And, for a need, you see I can play the match-maker.
She that is but one and professeth so many,
May well be termed a wise woman, if there be any. *Exit*

ACT 3, SCENE 2

Enter [*Master*] BOYSTER

Boyster Why run away and leave my wench behind? I'll back. What have warrants and pursuivants to do with me? With me? Why should I budge? Why should I wear mask or vizard? If lords or ladies offend, let lords and ladies answer. Let me better bethink me. Why should I play at Hob-man blind? Hum, why marry *in tenebris*? Ha! Is there no trick in it? If my grannam should make me a younger brother now, and instead of Luce pop me off with some broken commodity, I were finely served.

Most sure I am to be in for better and worse,
But with whom, heaven and my grannam knows.

Enter LUCE 2, [*unmasking*]

Luce 2 [*aside*] I am stolen out of doors to see if I can meet my husband, with whom I purpose to make some sport, ere I suddenly disclose myself. What's he?

Boyster [*aside*] Heyday, what have we here? An hobbledehoy? – Come hither, you.

Luce 2 [*aside*] 'Tis Mistress Luce's husband; I'll not leave him thus.

Boyster What art thou?

Luce 2 Do you not know me?

Boyster That mask and robe I know.

Luce 2 I hope so, or else I were in a woe case.

Boyster That mask, that gown, I married.

Luce 2 Then you have no reason but to enjoy both them and me too, and so you are like; I should be loath to divorce man and wife.

Boyster I am fooled. But what cracked ware are you, forsooth?

Luce 2 I belong to the old gentlewoman of the house.

Boyster I'll set her house on fire! I am finely bobbed.

Luce 2 But I hope you will not bob me.

Boyster No I shall warrant thee. What art thou, girl or boy?

Luce 2 Both and neither: I was a lad last night, but in the morning I was conjured into a lass, and being a girl now, I shall be translated to a boy anon. Here's all I can at this time say for myself. Farewell. [*Exit*]

Boyster Yes, and be hanged withal. Oh, for some gunpowder to blow up this witch, this she-cat, this damned sorceress! Oh, I could tear her to fitters with my teeth! Yet I must be patient and put up all, lest I be made a jeer to such as know me. Fooled by a boy! Go to, of all the rest, the girl Luce must not know it. *Exit*

ACT 3, SCENE 3

Enter [*severally*] CHARTLEY *and* [SERVING-MAN 1], *meeting* LUCE

Chartley So, now am I the same man I was yesterday. Who can say I was disguised? Or who can distinguish my condition now? Or read in my face whether I be a married man or a bachelor?

Luce Who's that?

Chartley Luce.

Luce Sweet husband, is it you?

Chartley The news?

Luce Never so frighted in my days.

Chartley What's become of the lord and the lady?

Luce The lord fled after you; the lady stayed, who,

masked and half unready, ran fast after her poor affrighted husband. Now all's quiet.

Chartley This storm is then well past, and now convey yourself home as privately as you can, and see you make this known to none but your father.

Luce I am your wife and servant. *[Exit]*

Chartley This name of Luce hath been ominous to me. One Luce I should have married in the country; and just the night before, a toy took me in the head, and mounting my horse, I left capons, ducks, geese, poultry, wild-fowl, father and bride and all, and posted up to London, where I have ever since continued bachelor. Till now. And now –

Enter GRATIANA *in haste,* [SERVING-MAN 2] *before her, and* TABOR *after her*

Gratiana Nay, on! I prithee, fellow, on! My father will wonder where I have been visiting. Now, what had I forgot? Tabor, there's money. Go to the goldsmith's, bid him send me my fan and make a quick return. On, fellow, on.

[*Exeunt* GRATIANA *and* SERVING-MAN 2

Tabor Her fan at the goldsmith's? Now had I forgot to ask her his name or his sign. But I will after to know. [*Exit*]

Chartley Sirrah, go call me back that serving-man,
And ask him what's the gentlewoman's name.

Serving-man 1 I shall. Ho! You! Friend! You!

[*Re-enter* TABOR]

Tabor Who's that calls?

Serving-man 1 'Twas I.

Tabor Your business? You should be one, though not of my cognizance, yet of my condition: a serving-creature, as I take it. Pray, what's your will with me?

Serving-man 1 Pray, sir, what might I call that gentlewoman on whom you were attendant?

Tabor You may call her what you please, but if you call her otherwise than in the way of honesty, you may perchance hear on't.

Serving-man 1 Nay, be not offended. I say, what do you call her?

Tabor Why, sir, I call her as it shall best please me: sometimes young lady, sometimes young mistress. And what hath any man to do with that?

Chartley Are you so captious, sirrah? What's her name? Speak and be brief.

Tabor Aye, marry, sir. You speak to purpose, and I can resolve you. Her name is Gratiana. But all this while I have forgot my mistress' fan. *Exit*

Chartley Gratiana! Oft have I heard of her but saw her not till now. 'Tis a pretty wench, a very pretty wench; nay, a very, very, very pretty wench. But what a rogue am I of a married man? Nay, that have not been married this six hours and to have my shittle wits run a-wool-gathering already? What would poor Luce say if she should hear of this? I may very well call her poor Luce, for I cannot presume of five pounds to her portion. What a coxcomb was I, being a gentleman and well derived, to match into so beggarly a kindred? What needed I to have grafted in the stock of such a choke-pear, and such a goodly popering as this to escape me? Escape me, said I? If she do, she shall do it narrowly. But I am married already, and therefore it is not possible, unless I should make away my wife, to compass her. Married! Why, who knows it? I'll outface the priest, and then there is none but she and her father, and their evidence is not good in law. And if they put me in suit, the best is, they are poor and cannot follow it. Aye, marry, sir, a man may have some credit by such a wife as this. I could like this marriage well, if a man might change away his wife still as he is aweary of her and cope her away like a bad commodity. If every new moon a man might have a new wife, that's every year a dozen. But this "Till death us depart" is tedious. I will go a-wooing to her, I will. But how shall I do for jewels and tokens? Luce hath mine in her custody, money and all. Tush, I'll juggle them from her well enough. See, here she comes.

Enter LUCE *and* LUCE'S FATHER

Luce Here is my husband; I pray move him in it.

Luce's father It toucheth both our reputations nearly;
For by his oft repair, now whilst the marriage
Is kept from public knowledge, your good name

May be by neighbours hardly censur'd of.

Chartley Th'art sad, th'art sad, Luce. What, melancholy already, ere thou hast had good cause to be merry and knew'st what sport was?

Luce I have great reason, when my name is toss'd
In every gossip's mouth, and made a byword
Unto such people as it least concerns.
Nay, in my hearing, as they pass along,
Some have not spar'd to brand my modesty,
Saying, "There sits she whom young Chartley keeps.
There hath he ent'red late, betimes gone forth".
Where I with pride was wont to sit before,
I'm now with shame sent blushing from the door.

Chartley Alas, poor fool, I am sorry for thee; but yet cannot help thee, as I am a gentleman. Why say, Luce, thou losest now forty shillings worth of credit; stay but a time, and it shall bring thee in a thousand pounds worth of commodity.

Luce's father Son, son, had I esteem'd my profit more
Than I have done my credit, I had now
Been many thousands richer. But, you see,
Truth and good dealing bear an humble sail.
That little I enjoy, it is with quiet,
Got with good conscience, kept with good report;
And that I still shall labour to preserve.

Chartley But, do you hear me?

Luce's father Nothing I'll hear that tends unto the ruin
Of mine or of my daughter's honesty.
Shall I be held a broker to lewd lust
Now, in my wane of years?

Chartley Will you but hear me?

Luce's father Not in this case. I that have liv'd thus long,
Reported well, esteem'd a welcome guest
At every burthen'd table, there respected,
Now to be held a pander to my daughter?
That I should live to this!

Chartley But hark you, father.

Luce's father A bawd to mine own child!

Chartley Father!

Luce's father To my sweet Luce!

Chartley Father!

Luce's father Deal with me like a son. Then call me father.
I that have had the tongues of every man
Ready to crown my reputation;
The hands of all my neighbours to subscribe
To my good life; and such as could not write,
Ready, with palsy and unlettered fingers,
To set their scribling marks –

Chartley Why, father-in-law!

Luce's father Thou hadst a mother, Luce; 'tis woe with me
To say thou hadst but hast not. A kind wife
And a good nurse she was. She, had she liv'd
To hear my name thus canvass'd and thus toss'd
Seven years before she died, I had been a widower
Seven years before I was. Heaven rest her soul,
She is in heaven I hope. (*Wipes his eyes*)

Chartley Why, so now, these be good words. I knew these storms would have a shower and then they would cease. Now, if your anger be over, hear me.

Luce's father Well, say on, son.

Chartley Stay but a month; 'tis but four weeks. Nay, 'tis February, the shortest month of the year, and in that time I shall be at full age, and, the land being entailed, my father can disinherit me of nothing. Is your spleen down now? Have I satisfied you? [*aside*] Well, I see you choleric hasty men are the kindest when all is done. Here's such wetting of handkerchiefs. He weeps to think of his wife, she weeps to see her father cry. – Peace, fool, we shall else have thee claim kindred of the Woman Killed with Kindness.

Luce's father Well, son, my anger's past; yet I must tell you,
It grieves me that you should thus slight it off,
Concerning us in such a dear degree.
In private be it spoke, my daughter tells me,
She's both a wife and maid. contradiction in terms

Chartley That may be helped.
Now, Luce, your father's pacified, will you be pleased? I would endure a quarter's punishment for thee, and wilt not thou suffer a poor month's penance for me? 'Tis but eight and twenty days, wench; thou shalt fare well all the time, drink well, eat well, lie well. Come, one word of comfort at the latter end of the day.

Luce Yours is my fame, mine honour, and my heart,
Link'd to your pleasure, and shall never part.

Chartley Gramercy, wench; thou shalt wear this chain no longer for that word. I'll multiply the links in such order that it shall have light to shine about thy neck oftener than it doth. This jewel, a plain Bristol stone, a counterfeit. How base was I, that coming to thee in the way of marriage, courted thee with counterfeit stones? Thou shalt wear right or none. Thou hast no money about thee, Luce?

Luce Yes, sir; I have the hundred pounds that you gave me to lay up last.

Chartley Fetch it. [*Exit* LUCE] Let me see; how much branched satin goes to a petticoat? And how much wrought velvet to a gown? Then for a beaver for the city and a black bag for the country? [*Aside*] I'll promise her nothing, but if any such trifles be brought home, let her not thank me for them. –

[*Re-*]*enter* LUCE *with the bag*

Gramercy, Luce. Nay, go in, gravity and modesty, ten to one but you shall hear of me ere you see me again.

Luce's father I know you kind; impute my hasty language unto my rage, not me.

Chartley Why, do not I know you, and do not I know her? [*aside*] I doubt you'll wish shortly that I had never known either of you. – Now, what sayst thou, my sweet Luce?

Luce My words are yours, so is my life. I am now part of yourself, so made by nuptial vows.

Chartley [*aside*] What a pagan am I to practise such villany against this honest Christian! If Gratiana did not come into my thoughts, I should fall into a vein to pity her; but now that I talk of her, I have a tongue to woo her, tokens to win her. And that done, if I do not find a trick both to wear her and weary her, it may prove a piece of a wonder. – Thou seest, Luce, I have some store of crowns about me. There are brave things to be bought in the city; Cheapside and the Exchange afford variety and rarity. This is all I will say now, but thou mayest hear more of me hereafter.

[*Exeunt* CHARTLEY *and* SERVING-MAN 1]

Luce Heaven speed you where you go, sir. Shall we in?
Though not from scandal, we live free from sin.

Luce's father I'll in before. *Exit*

Enter Master BOYSTER

Boyster I'm still in love with Luce, and I would know
An answer more directly. Fie, fie, this love
Hangs on me like an ague, makes me turn fool,
Coxcomb and ass. Why should I love her, why?
A rattle-baby, puppet, a slight toy,
And now I could go to buffets with myself,
And cuff this love away. But see, that's Luce.

Luce I cannot shun him, but I'll shake him off.

Boyster Morrow.

Luce As much to you.

Boyster I'll use few words: canst love me?

Luce Deed, sir, no.

Boyster Why, then, farewell; the way I came, I'll go. *Exit*

Luce This is no tedious courtship; he's soon answer'd.
So should all suitors else be, were they wise;
For being repulsed, they do but waste their days
In thankless suits and superficial praise.

[*Re-*]*enter* BOYSTER

Boyster Swear that thou wilt not love me.

Luce Not, sir, for any hate I ever bear you,
Or any foolish pride or vain conceit;
Or that your feature doth not please mine eye,
Or that you are not a brave gentleman.
But for concealed reasons I am forc'd
To give you this cold answer, and to swear
I must not. Then with patience, pray, forbear.

Boyster Even farewell then. *Exit*

Luce The like to you, and save your hopes in me.
Heaven grant you your best wishes; all this strife
Will end itself, when I am known a wife. [*Exit*]

ACT 4, SCENE 1

Enter SIR HARRY, *Master* HARINGFIELD *and* GRATIANA

Sir Harry I am satisfied, good Master Haringfield, touching your friend; and since I see you have left his dangerous company, I limit you to be a welcome guest unto my table.

Haringfield You have been always noble.

Enter TABOR

Sir Harry Tabor, the news with thee.

Tabor May it please the right worshipful to understand that there are some at the gate who dance a turn or two without and desire to be admitted to speak with you within.

Sir Harry The scholar, is it not?

Tabor Nay, sir, there are two scholars, and they are spouting Latin one against the other. And in my simple judgement the stranger is the better scholar and is somewhat too hard for Sir Boniface, for he speaks louder, and that, you know, is ever the sign of the most learning. And he also hath a great desire to serve your worship.

Sir Harry Two scholars! My house hath not place for two.
Thus it shall be. Tabor, admit them both. [*Exit* TABOR]
We, though unlearned, will hear them two

dispute, and he that of the two seems the best read, shall be received, the other quite cashiered.

Haringfield In that you show but justice; in all persons merit should be regarded.

Re-enter TABOR, *ushering* SIR BONIFACE *and* SENCER, *disguised like a pedant*

Sir Boniface *Venerabiles magistri:*
Absint vobis capistri.

Sencer *Et tu, domini calve,*
Iterum atque iterum salve.
Amo amas amavi,
Sweet lady, heaven save ye.

Sir Harry This approves him to be excellent, but I thank my breeding I understand not a word. You tongue-men, you whose wealth lies in your brains, not in your budgets, hear me. Be it known, my house affords room for one schoolmaster, but not for more. And I am thus resolved: take you that side, gentle Sir Boniface; and, sir, possess you that. He of you two in arguing proves the best, to him will I subscribe. Are you agreed?

Sir Boniface *Nec animo, nec corde, nec utroque.*

Sencer No more of that *nec corde*, noble knight; he wishes you *nec corde*, think of that.

Sir Harry A cord about my neck, Sir Boniface?
Speak, do you use me well?

Sir Boniface *Domine, cur rogas?*

Sencer Is this to be endured, to call a knight
Cur, rogue and ass?

Sir Harry I find myself abused.

Haringfield Yet patience, good Sir Harry, and hear more. Pray, Sir Boniface, of what university were you of?

Sir Boniface I was student in Brasenose.

Haringfield A man might guess so much by your pimples. And of what place were you?

Sencer *Petrus dormit securus*; I was, sir, of Peterhouse.

Sir Boniface *Natus eram* in Woxford, and I proceeded in Oxford.

Sencer *Est mihi bene nostrum*, thou wouldest say, in Gotham. For my part, Sir Harry, I can read service and, marry, *que genus et flexum*, though I go in genes fustian, *scalpellum et charta*, I was not brought up at plough and cart. I can teach *qui mihi* and neither laugh nor tee-hee; *sed as in presente*, if your worship at this present, *Iste Ista Istud*, will do me any good to give me *legem pone* in gold or in money, *piper atque papaver*, I'll deserve it with any labour.

Haringfield But when go you to dispute?

Sir Boniface *Nominativo hic prediculus*, his words are most ridiculous. But *tu*, thou, *qui*, the which, *deridest* those that be rich, *construe hanc sententiam*, construe me this sentence. *Est modus in rebus, sunt certi denique fines.*

Sencer *Est modus in rebus*, there is mud in the rivers; *Sunt certi denique fines*, and certain little fishes.

Sir Harry I warrant you, he hath his answer ready.

Sir Boniface *Dii boni boni.*

Haringfield He'll give you more bones than those to gnaw on, Sir Boniface.

Sencer Καρτερε Μουσοτροφος, πολυφιλτατε φιλε ποετες, Της λογικης ρετωρ, ουχ ελαχιστε σοφων. That is as much as to say, in our *materna lingua*, I will make you, Sir Boniface, confess yourself an ass in English, speak open and broad words for want of Latin, and *denique*, instruct me to resolve such questions as I shall ask you in our modern tongue.

Sir Harry Confess himself an ass? Speak obscene words? After entreat thee to resolve thy questions? Do that; possess the place.

Sencer *Di do* and *dum*;
No more words but mum.

Sir Boniface Noble Sir Harry, *numquam sic possit*?

Sir Harry Sir Boniface is sick already and calls for a posset; no marvel, being so threatened.

Sencer You, Boniface, decline me "I am a no" after the first conjugation, *amo amavi*, *vocito vocitavi*, *titubo titubavi*.

Sir Boniface I am not the preceptor to a pupil, but can decline it. Mark, Sir Timothy: "I am a no" …

Sencer *Bene*, *bene*.

Sir Boniface "I am an as" …

Sencer Most true, most true.

Vos estis, ut ego sum testis,
That what he confessed
Is as true as the *pestis*.

Sir Harry This scholar works by magic! He hath made him confess himself an ass!

Sir Boniface *Per has meas manus,*
Vir, tu es insanus.

Sencer I'll make him fret worse yet. Sir Boniface, *quid est grammatica*?

Sir Boniface *Grammatica est ars.*

Sir Harry Fie, fie! No more of these words, good Sir Boniface.

Sencer Attend again. Proceed me with this verse of reverend Cato: *Si deus est animus –*

Sir Boniface *Nobis ut carmina dicunt –*

Tabor Di – cunt, quotha! Out on him for a beastly man!

Sir Harry I would not have him teach my children so for more than I am worth.

Sir Boniface Oh! But reverend Sir Harry, you must *subaudi*.

Sir Harry I'll never be so bawdy whilst I live, nor any of mine I hope.

Sir Boniface Oh! *Propria quæ maribus.*

Sir Harry Aye, Boniface, is it those marrowbones that make you talk so broadly?

Sir Boniface *Venerabilis vir, homo ille est ebrius.*

Sir Harry What doth he mean by that?

Sencer He saith, "I can speak Hebrew".

Sir Harry I believe't. But if Sir Boniface still con these lessons, he'll speak the French tongue perfect.

Sencer Now, to the last; I'll task Sir Boniface but with an easy question. –Tell me, sir: what's Latin for this earth?

Sir Boniface Facile and easy, more fit for the pupil than the preceptor. What's Latin for this earth? *Tellus.*

Sencer Tell you? No sir, it belongs to you to tell me.

Sir Boniface I say *tellus* is Latin for the earth.

Sencer And I say, I will not tell you what is Latin for the earth, unless you yield me victor.

Sir Harry You have no reason. Good Sir Timothy, the place is yours.

Haringfield He hath deserved it well.

Sencer But I'll deserve it better. Why, this fellow
Is frantic. You shall hear me make him speak
Idly and without sense.
(*He whispers to* SIR HARRY [*and* TABOR]
I'll make him say,
His nose was husband to a queen.

Sir Harry Sir Timothy, not possible.

Tabor He will not speak it for shame.

Sencer That you shall hear. [*To* SIR BONIFACE] *Magister* Boniface –

Sir Boniface *Quid ais, domine* Timothy?

Sencer Who was Pasiphae's husband, Queen of Crete?

Sir Boniface Who knows not that? Why, Minos was her

husband.

Sencer That his nose was! Did I not tell you so?

Sir Boniface I say that *Minos* was.

Sencer That his nose was! Ha, ha!

Sir Harry I'll not believe it.
Sir Boniface, there are a brace of angels;
You are not for my turn. – Sir Timothy,
You are the man shall read unto my daughter
The Latin tongue, in which I am ignorant. –
[*To* SIR BONIFACE]
Confess yourself an ass, speak bawdy words,
And after to talk idly! Hence, away!
You shall have my good word, but not my pay!

Sir Boniface *Opus est usus*. Sir Timothy, you abuse us.
I swear by a noun, had I thy hose down,
Qui que quod, I would so smoke thee with the rod,
Ille Illa Illud, until I fetched blood.
But, *Nobiles valete*, remain in *quiete*.
[*Exeunt* SIR BONIFACE *and* TABOR]

Sir Harry Sir Timothy, there is some gold in earnest. I like you well; take into your tuition my daughter Gratiana.

[*Re-enter* TABOR]

The news, Tabor.

Tabor Of another gallant, noble sir, that pretends to have business, both with you and my mistress.

Sir Harry Admit him.

Enter CHARTLEY *very gallant,* [*carrying a letter*]

Tabor — *Lusty Juventus*, will it please you to draw near?

Chartley — Noble knight, whil'st you peruse that [*hands* SIR HARRY *the letter*], sweet lady, tell me how you like this. (*Kisses her*)

Gratiana — You press so suddenly upon me, sir, I know not what to answer.

Sencer — [*aside*] Mad Chartley! What makes Desperation here?

Chartley — To the word Wooer, let me add the name Speeder. My father hath written to your father, and the cause of his writing at this present is to let you understand that he fears you have lived a maid too long. And therefore to prevent all diseases incident to the same, as the greensickness and others, he sent me like a skilful physician to take order with you against all such maladies. If you will not credit me, list but how fervently my father writes in my behalf.

Sir Harry — [*reading*] "He is my only son, and she I take as your only daughter; what should hinder, then, to make a match between them?" Well, 'tis well, 'tis good, I like it. "I will make her jointure three hundred pounds a year".

Chartley — How say you by that, sweet lady, three hundred pounds a year and a proper man to boot?

Sir Harry — All's good, I like it. Welcome Master Chartley. – Thou, Gratiana, art no child of mine unless thou bidst him welcome. – This I presume to be your father's hand?

Chartley [*aside*] But I'll be sworn he never writ it.

Sir Harry And this his seal at arms?

Chartley Or else I understand it very poorly. – But, lady, in earnest of further acquaintance, receive this chain, these jewels, hand and heart.

Sir Harry Refuse no chain nor jewels, heart nor hand, but in exchange of these bestow thyself, thine own dear self upon him.

Gratiana Myself on him, whom I till now I ne'er saw?
Well, since I must, your will's to me a law.

Sencer [*aside*] Nay, then, 'tis time to speak. Shall I stand here, waiting like a coxcomb, and see her given away before my face? – Stay your hand, Sir Harry, and let me claim my promise.

Sir Harry My promise I'll perform, Sir Timothy;
You shall have all your wages duly paid.

Sencer I claim fair Gratiana by your promise.
No more Sir Timothy, but Sencer now. [*Unmasks*]
You promis'd me when you receiv'd my service,
And with your liberal hand did wage my stay,
T'endow me freely with your daughter's love.
That promise now I claim.

Sir Harry Mere cozenage, knavery.
I tied myself to no conditions,
In which such guile is practis'd. Come, son Chartley,
To cut off all disasters incident
To these proceedings, we will solemnise
These nuptial rites with all speed possible.

Chartley Farewell, good Sir Timothy; farewell, learned Sir Timothy. *Exeunt* [*all but* SENCER

Sencer Why, and farewell, learned Sir Timothy,
For now Sir Timothy and I am two.
Boast on, brag on, exalt, exalt thyself,
Swim in a sea of pleasure and content
Whilst my bark suffers wreck. I'll be reveng'd,
Chartley. I'll cry *vindicta* for this scorn,
Next time thou gorest, it must be with thy horn. *Exi*

ACT 4, SCENE 2

Enter Master BOYSTER

Boyster I am mad and know not at what.
I could swagger but know not with whom.
I am at odds with myself and know not why.
I shall be pacified and cannot tell when.
I would fain have a wife but cannot tell where.
I would fasten on Luce but cannot tell how.
How; where; when; why; whom; what.
Feeding sure makes me lean and fasting fat.

Enter LUCE *and* JOSEPH

Luce Not all this while once see me?

Joseph His occasions perhaps enforce his absence.

Luce His occasions!

Unless he find occasion of new love,
What could enforce such absence from his spouse?
Am I grown foul and black since my espousals?
It should not seem so, for the shop is daily
Custom'd with store of chapmen such as come
To cheapen love. O no, I am myself,
But Chartley, he is changed.

Joseph [*spotting* BOYSTER] You know that gentleman?

Luce Escape him if thou canst.

Boyster He cannot; I arrest you.

Luce At whose suit?

Boyster Not at mine own, that's dashed. I love thee not.
Thou art a Spaniard, gipsy, a mere blackamoor.
Again, I say, I love thee not.

Luce [*aside*] *A* blackamoor, a gipsy?
Sure I am chang'd indeed, and that's the cause
My husband left me so. This gentleman
Once term'd me beautiful. – How look I, Joseph?

Joseph As well as ere you did: fat, fresh, and fair.

Boyster You lie, boy; pocket that [*offers him money*], and now be gone.

Joseph And what shall then become of my mistress?

Boyster I'll wait upon your mistress.

Luce I know you will not wait on such a gipsy.

Boyster Yes Luce, on such a gipsy. Boy, *abi, abi*.

Joseph Abide, sir? You need not fear that; I have no purpose to leave her.

Boyster Now you are going to the wedding-house.
You are bid to be a bridesmaid, are you not?

Luce What wedding sir, or whose?

Boyster Why, Chartley's. Luce, hath he been thy friend so long and would not bid thee to wait on his bride? Why lookst thou red and pale, and both, and neither?

Luce To Master Chartley's bridals? Why, to whom
Should he be married?

Boyster To Grace of Gracious Street.

Luce To Gratiana?
Beshrew you, sir. You do not use me well
To buzz into mine ears these strange untruths.
I tell you, sir, 'tis as impossible
That they two should match, as earth and heaven to meet.

Boyster You'll not believe it? Pray then, hark within
The nuptial music echoing to their joys.
But you give credit to no certainties:
I told you but a tale, a lie, a fable,
A monstrous, a notorious idle untruth,
That you were black, and that I lov'd you not,
And you could credit that.

Enter SIR HARRY, HARINGFIELD, CHARTLEY *leading* GRATIANA *by the arm,* TABOR *and attendants*

Who's tell-truth now?
Know you that man, or know you that fine virgin,
Whom by the arm he leads?

Luce I'll not endure't. [*To* CHARTLEY] Heaven give you joy, sir.

Chartley I thank you. Luce? *She faints*

Sir Harry Look to the maid. She faints! BOYSTER *holds her up*

Chartley Grace, come not near her, Grace.
Father, keep off; on, gentlemen, apace.
She's troubled with the falling sickness, for oft hath she fallen before me.

Sir Harry Nay, if it be no otherwise, on gentlemen. Let those with her strive to recover her. Keep off, the disease is infectious.

Chartley If it were in a man, it were nothing; but the falling sickness in a woman is dangerous. –

Enter LUCE'S FATHER

[*aside*] My t'other father-in-law! Now shall I be utterly shamed. If he assure to know me, I'll outface him.

Luce's father Son, you're well met.

Chartley How, fellow?

Luce's father I cry you mercy, sir. [*Stands aside*]

Chartley No harm done, friend; no harm done.

Exeunt [SIR HARRY, HARINGFIELD, CHARTLEY, GRATIANA, TABOR *and attendants*]

Luce's father [*aside*] If he, he could not but have known me there;
Yet he was wondrous like him.

Boyster How cheer you, Luce? Whence grew this passion?

Luce Pardon me, sir; I do not know myself.
I am apt to swoon, and now the fit is past me,
I thank you for your help. Is Master Chartley
Vanished so soon?

Boyster Yes, and to supply his place, see where thy father comes.

Luce's father [*aside*] He hath not such a suit; besides this gallant
Led by the arm a bride, a lusty bride.
How much might I have wrong'd the gentleman
By craving his acquaintance. This it is
To have dim eyes. – [*To* LUCE] Why looks my daughter sad?
[*To* BOYSTER] I cry you mercy, sir. I saw not you.

Boyster I would I had not seen you at this time neither.
Farewell. *Exit*

Luce If he be gone, then let me vent my grief.
Father, I am undone.

Luce's father Forbid it, heaven.

Luce Disgrac'd, despis'd, discarded and cast off.

Luce's father How, mine own child?

Luce My husband! Oh, my husband!

Luce's father What of him?

Luce Shall I the shower of all my grief at once
Pour out before you? Chartley, once my husband,
Hath left me to my shame. Him and his bride
I met within few minutes.

Luce's father Sure 'twas they!
I met them too. 'Twas he, base villain, Jew.
I'll to the wedding board, and tell him so.

I'll do't, as I am a man.

Luce Be not so rash.

Luce's father I'll live and die upon him;
He's a base fellow, so I'll prove him too.
Joseph, my sword.

Luce This rashness will undo us.

Luce's father I'll have my sword.
It hath been twice in France, and once in Spain,
With John-a-Gaunt. When I was young like him
I had my wards, and foins, and quarter-blows,
And knew the way into St. George's Fields
Twice in a morning. Tuttle, Finsbury,
I knew them all. I'll to him. Where's my sword?

Luce Or leave this spleen, or you will overthrow
Our fortunes quite. Let us consult together,
What we were best to do.

Luce's father I'll make him play at leap-frog. Well, I hear thee.

Luce I cannot prove our marriage, it was secret,
And he may find some cavil in the law.

Luce's father I'll to him with no law, but Stafford Law.
I'll ferret the false boy. Nay, on, good Luce.

Luce Part of your spleen, if you would change to counsel,
We might revenge us better.

Luce's father Well I hear thee.

Luce To claim a public marriage at his hands
We want sufficient proof; and then the world
Will but deride our folly, and so add
Double disgrace unto my former wrong.

To law with him, he hath a greater purse
And nobler friends. How then to make it known?

Luce's father Is this his damask'd kirtle fringed with gold,
His black bag, and his beaver? 'Tis well yet
I have a sword.

Luce And I have a project in my brain begot,
To make his own mouth witness to the world
My innocence and his incontinence.
Leave it to me. I'll clear myself from blame;
Though I the wrong, yet he shall reap the shame. *Exeun*

ACT 4, SCENE 3

Enter SENCER [*disguised*] *like a serving-man*

Sencer Now or never! Look about thee, Sencer; tomorrow is the marriage day, which to prevent lies not within the compass of my apprehension. Therefore I have thus disguised myself, to go to the looming woman's, the fortune-teller's, the anything, the nothing. This over against Mother Redcap's is her house. I'll knock. [*Knocks*]

Enter LUCE 2 *in her boy's shape*

Luce 2 Who's there? What would you have?

Sencer I would speak with the wise gentlewoman of the house.

Luce 2 Oh, belike you have lost somewhat?

Sencer You are in the wrong, sweet youth.

Luce 2 I am somewhat thick of hearing. Pray, speak out.

Sencer [*shouting*] I say, I have not lost anything, but wit and time; and neither of those she can help me to.

Luce 2 Then you belike are crossed in love, and come to know what success you shall have?

Sencer Thou hast hit it, sweet lad; thou hast hit it.

Luce 2 What is it you say, sir?

Sencer [*shouting*] Thou hast hit it.

Luce 2 I pray, come in, I'll bring you to my mistress. [*Exeunt*]

Enter LUCE *and* JOSEPH

Luce This is the house. Knock, Joseph; my business craves dispatch.

Joseph Now am I as angry as thou art timorous; and now to vent on the next thing I meet – Oh, 'tis the door. *Knocks*

Re-enter LUCE 2

Luce 2 Who's there? What are you?

Luce A maid and a wife.

Luce 2 [*aside*] And that would grieve any wench to be so, I know that by myself, not Luce.

Luce Boy, where's your mistress?

Luce 2 In some private talk with a gentleman.

I'll fetch her to you presently. *Exi*

Luce If she can see me not, I am but dead;
I shall be made a byword to the world,
The scorn of women, and my father's shame.

Enter the WISE WOMAN, SENCER [*and* LUCE 2]

Wise Woman You tell me your name is Sencer? I knew it before. And that Chartley is to be married? I could have told it you.

Luce 2 [*aside*] Married tomorrow! O me!

Sencer Aye, but you tell me that Chartley before tomorrow shall be disappointed of his wife. Make that good, thou shalt have twenty angels.

Wise Woman I'll do't. Stand aside; I'll have but a word or two with this gentlewoman, and I am for you presently. [SENCER *withdraws*]

Luce Oh! Mother, mother. *They whispe*

Luce 2 [*aside*] My husband marry another wife tomorrow? Oh, changeable destiny! No sooner married to him, but instantly to lose him. Nor death it grieves me so much that I am a wife, but that I am a maid too. To carry one of them well is as much as any is bound to do, but to be tied to both is more than flesh and blood can endure.

Wise Woman Well, trust to me, and I will set all things straight.

Enter [*Master*] BOYSTER

Boyster Where's this witch, this hag, this beldam, this wizard? An have I found thee, thus then will I tear, mumble and maul thee.

Wise Woman [*to* SENCER] Help, help, and if you be a gentleman.

Sencer Forbear this rudeness. He that touches her
Draws against me.

Boyster Against you, sir? Apply thou; that shall be tried. [*They fight*]

All Help, help! Part them! Help!

Sencer With patience, hear her speak.

Boyster Now trot, now grannam, what canst thou say for thyself? What, Luce here? Be patient and put up then; she must not see the end.

Sencer Then truce of all sides. If we come for counsel,
Let us with patience hear't.

Luce Then first to me.

Wise Woman [*to* LUCE] You would prevent young Chartley's marriage? You shall. Hark in your ear. [*Whispers*]

Luce It pleaseth me.

Wise Woman [*to* SENCER] You forestall Gratiana's wedding? 'Tis but thus. [*Whispers*]

Sencer I'll do't.

Wise Woman [*to* BOYSTER] You would enjoy Luce as your wife, and lie with her tomorrow night? Hark in your ear. [*Whispers*]

Boyster *Fiat.*

Wise Woman [*to* BOYSTER] Away, you shall enjoy her. [*to* LUCE] You are married, Luce; away! [*to*

SENCER] You shall see Chartley discarded from Gratiana; Sencer, be gone. [*To all*] And if I fail in any of these or the rest, I lay myself open to all your displeasures.

Boyster Farewell till soon.

Wise Woman You know your meeting-place.

All We do.

Wise Woman You shall report me wise and cunning too.

[*Exeunt all except* LUCE 2

Luce 2 I'll add one night more to the time I have said.
I have not many I hope to live a maid. *Exit*

ACT 4, SCENE 4

Enter SIR BONIFACE, *and* TABOR
[*carrying*] *a napkin and a trencher of broken meat*

Tabor Fie, fie! What a time of trouble is this. Tomorrow, tomorrow is my mistress to be married, and we serving-men are so puzzled.

Sir Boniface The dinner's half done, and before I say Grace
And bid the old knight and his guest proface,
A medicine from your trencher, good Master Tabor,
As good a man as e're was Sir Sabre.
Well, think it no shame: men of learning and wit
Say study gets a stomach. Friend Tabor, a bit.

Tabor Lick clean, good Sir Boniface, and save the scraper

a labour.

Enter SENCER [*disguised*] *like a serving-man*

Sir Boniface But soft, let me ponder;
Know you him that comes yonder?

Tabor Most heartily welcome. Would you speak with any here?

Sencer Pray, is the young gentleman of the house at leisure?

Tabor Mean you the bridegroom, Master Chartley?

Sencer I have a letter for him. You seem to be a gentleman yourself; acquaint him with my attendance, and I shall rest yours in all good offices.

Tabor Sir Boniface, pray, keep the gentleman company. I will first acquaint your lips with the virtue of the cellar. [*Exit*]

Sir Boniface *Adesdem*, come near, and taste of our beer.
Welcome, *sine dole,* for *puntis te vole*.

Sencer When I taste of your liquor,
Gramercy, Master Vicar.

[*Re-*]*enter* TABOR *with a napkin and a bowl of beer*

Tabor Most heartily welcome. Your courtesy, I beseech you; ply it off, I entreat you. Pray, Sir Boniface, keep the gentleman company, till I acquaint my young master with his business. *Exit*

Sir Boniface Tabor, I shall. (*They dissemble one to another*) *Beso las manos.*

Sencer *À votre service.*

Enter HARINGFIELD

Haringfield Ha, what art thou?

Sencer A hanger on, if it please you.

Haringfield And I, a shaker off. I'll not bear your gallows; you shall not hang on me.

Enter CHARTLEY *with his napkin as from dinner*

Oh, Master Bridegroom.

Chartley Gentlemen, the ladies call upon you to dance. They will be out of measure displeased, if dinner being done, you be not ready to lead them a measure.

Haringfield Indeed, women love not to be scanted of their measure.

Chartley Fie, Sir Boniface, have you forgot yourself? Whilst you are in the hall, there's never a whetstone for their wits in the parlour.

Sir Boniface I will enter and set an edge upon their *ingenies.*

[*As* SIR BONIFACE *and* HARINGFIELD *exeunt,* SENCER *hands* CHARTLEY *a letter*]

Chartley To me, sir? From whom? A letter "To her most

dear, most loving, most kind friend Master Chartley; these be delivered". Sure from some wench or other; I long to know the contents.

Sencer [*aside*] Now to cry quittance with you for my "Farewell, learned Sir Timothy".

Chartley Good news, as I live. There's for thy pains, my good Sir Pandarus [*gives him money*]. Hadst thou brought me word my father had turned up his heels, thou couldst scarcely have pleased me better. (*Reading*) "Though I disclaim the name of wife, of which I account myself altogether unworthy, yet let me claim some small interest in your love. This night I lie at the house where we were married – the Wise Woman's, I mean – where my maidenhead is to be rifled. Bid fair for it, and enjoy it. See me this night or never; so may you marrying Gratiana and loving me, have a sweet wife and a true friend. This night or never; your *quondam* wife, hereafter your poor sweetheart, no other, Luce." So when I am tired with Gratiana, that is, when I am past grace, with her I can make my rendezvous. I'll not slip this occasion, nor sleep till I see her. Thou art an honest lad, and mayst prove a good pimp in time. Canst thou advise me what colour I may have to compass this commodity?

Sencer Sir, she this night expects you, and prepares a costly banquet for you.

Chartley I'll go, although the devil and mischance look big.

Sencer Feign some news that such a piece of land is fallen to you, and you must instantly ride to take possession of it. Or, which is more probable, cannot you persuade them you have received a letter that your father lies a-dying?

Chartley You rogue, I would he did; but the name of that news is called, "too good to be true".

Sencer And that if ever you will see him alive, you must ride post into the country.

Chartley Enough! If ever I prove knight errant, thou shalt be mine own proper squire, for this. Thou hast fitted me with a plot. Do but wait here. Note how I will manage it. – [*Shouts*] Tabor, my horse, for I must ride tonight.

[*Re-enter* TABOR]

Tabor Tonight, sir?

Chartley So tell my bride and father, I have news that quite confounds my senses.

Enter SIR HARRY, GRATIANA *and* HARINGFIELD

Gratiana How, ride tonight, the marriage day tomorrow
And all things well provided for the feast?
Oh, tell me, sweet, why do you look so pale?

Chartley My father, oh, my father!

Gratiana What of him?

Sir Harry What of your father, son?

Chartley If ever I will hear his aged tongue
Preach to me counsel; or his palsy hand

Stroke my wild head and bless me; or his eyes
Drop tear by tear, which they have often done
At my misgoverned rioting youth;
What should I more, if ever I would see
The good old man alive? Oh, Oh!

Sencer [*aside*] Go thy ways, for thou shalt ha't.

Gratiana But do you mean to ride?

Chartley Aye, Grace, all this night.

Sencer [*aside*] Not all the night without alighting sure;
You'll find more in't than to get up and ride.

Haringfield The gentleman's riding boots and spurs. Why,
Tabor! [*Exit* TABOR]

Chartley Nay Grace, now's no time to stand on scrupulous parting. Knewest thou my business –

Sencer [*aside*] As she shall know it.

Chartley And how I mean this night to toil myself –

Sencer [*aside*] Marry, hang you, brock.

Chartley Thou would bemoan my travail.

Sencer [*aside*] I know 'twould grieve her.

Chartley You father, Grace, good Master Haringfield,
You sir, and all, pray for me, gentlemen,
That in this dark night's journey I may find
Smooth way, sweet speed and all things to my mind.

Sir Harry We'll see my son take horse.
Exeunt [CHARTLEY, SIR HARRY *and* HARINGFIELD]

Gratiana But I will stay.
I want the heart to see him post away.

Sencer Save you, gentlewoman. I have a message to deliver to one Mistress Gratiana. This should be the knight's house, her father.

Gratiana It is. The message that you have to her
You may acquaint me with, for I am one
That knows the inside of her thoughts.

Sencer Are you the lady?

Gratiana Sir, I am the poor gentlewoman.

Sencer There is a cunning woman dwells not far,
At Hoxton, lady, famous for her skill.
Besides some private talk that much concerns
Your fortunes in your love, she hath to show you
This night, if it shall please you walk so far
As to her house, an admirable suit
Of costly needlework, which if you please,
You may buy under-rate for half the value
It cost the making. About six o'clock
You may have view thereof, but otherwise
A lady that hath crav'd the sight thereof
Must have the first refusal.

Gratiana I'll not fail her.
My husband being this day rid from home,
My leisure fitly serves me. Thank your mistress.

Sencer At six o'clock.

Gratiana I will not fail the hour. *Exit*

Sencer Now to Sir Harry; his is the next place
To meet at Hoxton his fair daughter Grace. *Exit*

ACT 5, SCENE 1

Enter OLD MASTER CHARTLEY, *as new come out of the country to inquire after his son, and three or four serving-men with blue coats to attend him*

Old Chartley Good heaven! This London is a stranger grown and out of my acquaintance. This seven years I have not seen Paul's steeple or Cheap Cross.

Giles Sir.

Old Chartley Hast thou not made inquiry for my son?

Giles Yes, sir, I have asked about everywhere for him, but cannot hear of him.

Old Chartley Disperse yourselves; inquire about the taverns, ordinaries, bowl-alleys, tennis-courts, gaming-houses. For there, I fear, he will be found.

Giles But where shall we hear of your worship again?

Old Chartley At Grace Church by the Conduit, near Sir Harry.
But stay, leave off a while your bootless search.
Had ever man such a wild brain to his sorrow,
Of such small hope, who, when he should have married
A fair, a modest and a virtuous maid,
Rich and revenued well, and even the night
Before the marriage day, took horse, rode thence,
Whither heaven knows? Since the distracted virgin
Hath left her father's house, but neither found,
Yet in their search we have measured out much ground.

Enter SIR HARRY *and* SENCER [*disguised*]

Sencer Your worship will be there.

Sir Harry Yes, not to fail.
At half an hour past six, or before seven.

Sencer You shall not find us at six and at seven,
I'll warrant you. Good health to your worship. *Exit*

Sir Harry Farewell, good fellow.
At the Wise Woman's house, I know it well.
Perhaps she knows some danger touching me;
I'll keep mine hour.

Old Chartley Sir Harry, a hand, a hand; to baulk you it were sin.
I shall be bold to make your house mine inn.

Sir Harry Brother Chartley, I am glad to see you.

Old Chartley Methinks, Sir Harry, you look strangely on me,
And do not bid me welcome with an heart.

Sir Harry And blame me not to look amazedly
To see you here.

Old Chartley Why me?

Sir Harry Come, come; you're welcome,
And now I'll turn my strangeness to true joy.
I am glad to see you well and safe recover'd,
Of your late grievous sickness.

Old Chartley The strange amazed looks that you cast off
You put on me; and blame me not to wonder
That you should talk of sickness to sound men.
I thank my stars, I did not taste the grief
Of inward pain or outward malady

This seven years day.

Sir Harry But, by your favour, brother;
Then let me have my wonder back again.

Old Chartley Before I quite part with it, let me know
Why you the name of brother put upon me
In every clause; a name as strange to me,
As my recovered sickness.

Sir Harry You are pleasant,
And it becomes you well. Welcome again,
The rather you are come just to the wedding.

Old Chartley What wedding, sir?

Sir Harry That you should ask that question!
Why, of my daughter Grace.

Old Chartley Is Grace bestowed?
Of whom I pray?

Sir Harry Of whom, but of your son?
I wonder brother Chartley, and my friend,
You should thus play on me.

Old Chartley But by your favour,
Were you ten knights, Sir Harry, take me with you.
My son match with your daughter? My consent
Not worthy to be craved?

Sir Harry Nay, then I see,
You'll stir my patience. Know this forward match
Took its first birth from you.

Old Chartley From me?

Sir Harry From you.
[*Showing him a letter*] Peruse this letter; know you your own hand?

'Twas well that I reserv'd your hand a witness
Against your tongue. You had best deny the jointure
Of the three hundred pounds made to my daughter;
'Tis that I know you aim at. But your seal –

Old Chartley – shall not make me approve it! I deny
This seal for mine, nor do I vouch that hand.
Your daughter and the dower, letter and all,
I quite disclaim, Sir Harry. You much wrong me.

Sir Harry I can bear more than this. Heap wrong on wrong,
And I'll support it all. I for this time
Will cast my spleen behind me. And yet hear me:
This letter your son Chartley as from you
Delivered me. I like the motion well.

Old Chartley My spleen is further thrown aside than yours,
And I am full as patient. And yet hear me:
My son's contracted to another maid.
Nay, I am patient still. Yet that I writ
This letter, seal'd this impress, I deny.

Sir Harry Why, then the jack your hand did counterfeit?

Old Chartley Why, then he did so. Where's that unthrift, speak?

Sir Harry Some hour ago, he mounted and rid post
To give you visit whom he said lay sick
Upon your death-bed.

Old Chartley You amaze me, sir.
It is an ill presage; hereon I see
Your former salutation took its ground
To see me safe recovered of my sickness.

Sir Harry Indeed it did. Your welcome is a subject
I cannot use too oft; welcome again.
I am sorry you this night must sup alone,

For I am elsewhere call'd about some business,
Concerning what I know not. Hours run on;
I must to Hoxton. High time I were gone. *Exit*

Old Chartley Perhaps to the Wise Woman's. She may tell me
The fortunes of my son. This accident
Hath bred in me suspicion and strange fears.
I will not sup alone, but I protest
'Mongst some this night I'll play th'intruding guest. *Exeunt*

ACT 5, SCENE 2

Enter the WISE WOMAN, SENCER [*disguised*], LUCE, LUCE'S FATHER *and* LUCE 2

Wise Woman But will Sir Harry come?

Sencer Presume he will, and Chartley too.

Luce's father I'll have the knave by the ears.

Luce Nay, patience, sir; leave your revenge to me.

Enter Master BOYSTER

Boyster Grannam, I am come according to promise.

Wise Woman And welcome to the best hole that I have in Hoxton.

Boyster [*to* LUCE] Good even.

Luce Thanks, sir. A good even may it prove,
That each may reap the fruits of their own love.

Luce 2 [*aside*] That shall be my prayer too.

Boyster Come, what shall's do?

Wise Woman Withdraw, I'll place you all in several rooms,
where sit, see, but say nothing.
Exeunt [*all except* BOYSTER *and* LUCE'S FATHER

Enter TABOR *ushering* GRATIANA,
[*while* BOYSTER *and* LUCE'S FATHER *withdraw to upper-stage right*]

Tabor Here, sweet mistress; I know the place well,
Ever since I was here to know my fortune.

Gratiana Call me some half an hour hence. *Exit* [TABOR]

[*Re-*]*enter the* WISE WOMAN *and* LUCE 2

Wise Woman Your ladyship is most lovingly welcome.
A low stool for the gentlewoman, boy. [*Exit* LUCE 2
I made bold to send to you to take view
Of such a piece of work, as I presume
You have seldom seen the like.

Gratiana Of whose doing, I pray?

Wise Woman A friend of yours and mine. Please you withdraw.
I'll bring you to't.

Luce 2 [*within*] Mistress.

Wise Woman One calls. Sweet lady, I shall do you wrong,
But pray you think my little stay not long.
[*Exit* WISE WOMAN]

Enter SENCER, SIR HARRY *and* LUCE
[*while* GRATIANA *withdraws to upper-stage left*]

Sencer Here, sir, in this retiring chamber.

Sir Harry Gramercy, friend. How now; what's here to do?
A pretty wench and a close chamber too.

Luce That you have so much grac'd my mother's house,
With your desired presence, worthy knight,
Receive a poor maid's thanks. Who's there? A chair
And cushion for Sir Harry.

Sir Harry Thanks, most fair.
[*Sits down-stage left*]

Luce Please you but a few minutes here to stay
Till my return; I'll not be long away. [*Exit* LUCE]

Sencer The gentlewoman will wait on you
By and by, sir.

Sir Harry And I'll attend her, friend; [*Exit* SENCER]
Of all those doubts I long to know the end.

Enter LUCE 2 *and* OLD CHARTLEY

Luce 2 The knight you seek was here, or will be straight,
And if you be the man you name yourself,
You are most welcome, and you shall not back
Till you have seen Sir Harry.

Old Chartley Gentle youth,
I saw him enter here, and under privilege
Of his acquaintance made I bold to stay.

Luce 2 And you are welcome, sir; sit down, I pray.

[OLD CHARTLEY *sits down-stage right*

[*Enter the* WISE WOMAN, SENCER *and* LUCE]

Wise Woman Now they are placed in several rooms, that look into this one. Were Chartley come, we had all our company. [*Knocking*]

Sencer Hark, there's one knocks; 'tis Chartley on my life.

Luce One of you let him in, whilst I prepare me to entertain his coming.

[*Exit* WISE WOMAN *from one door, while* SENCER *meet*
CHARTLEY *at the other*

Enter CHARTLEY, *ushered in by* SENCER [*who then exits*]

Chartley What, old acquaintance Luce, not a word?
Yet some lip labour, if thou lovest me.

Gratiana [*aside*] My husband?

Sir Harry [*aside*] What, young Chartley?

Old Chartley [*aside*] How? My son?

Chartley Come, come, away with this wailing in woe.
If thou putst finger in the eye a little longer, I shall plunge in pain too presently.

Luce O husband, husband!

Gratiana [*aside*] Husband?

Chartley What sayst thou, my sweet wife?

Gratiana [*aside*] Wife? Oh, my heart!

Luce 2 [*aside*] In that name wife I claim a poor child's part.

Luce Oh, husband! How have you used me?

Chartley Nay, how do I mean to use thee, but as a man should use his wife?

Gratiana [*aside*] I hope he doth not mean to use her so.

Luce 2 [*aside*] I hope so too.

Boyster [*aside*] My grannam is a witch.

Chartley Nay, Luce, sweet wife, leave weeping if thou lov'st me.

Luce Oh, can you blame me, knowing that the fountain of all these springs took their first head from you? You know, you too will know, not three days since are past since we were married.

Gratiana [*aside*] Married? I can endure no longer.

Sir Harry [*aside*] It cannot be.

Old Chartley [*aside*] It is not possible.

Boyster [*aside*] I'll be even with thee for this, old grannam.

Luce And though we wanted witness upon earth,
Yet heaven bears record of our nuptial tie.

Chartley Tush, when we meet in heaven, let's talk of that.
Nay, come you ass, you fool; what's past is past.
Though man and wife, yet I must marry now
Another gallant. Here's thy letter, Luce,
And this night I intend to lodge with thee.

Luce 2 [*aside*] I'll scratch her eyes out first, although I love her.

Chartley Prethee, be merry.
I have made a gull of Grace, and old Sir Harry
Thinks me a great way off. I told the knight

My father lay a-dying, took post horse,
Rid out of Holborn, turn'd by Islington,
So hither, wench, to lodge all night with thee.

Luce 2 [*aside*] Here's one saith nay to that.

Old Chartley [*aside*] Was that your journey?

Chartley Why, I have too much of Grace already.

Boyster [*aside*] Thou hast no grace at all.

Chartley Nay, let's to bed.
If thou couldst but imagine how I love thee Luce, –

Luce How is it possible you can love me,
And go about to marry another?

Chartley Dost thou not know she's rich? Why, you fool, as soon as I have got her dower, it is but giving her a dram or a pill to purge melancholy to make her turn up her heels. And then with all that wealth, come I to live with thee, my sweet rascal.

Gratiana [*advancing*] She thanks you and is much beholding to you.

Chartley I am betrayed!

Gratiana Art thou my suitor? Would'st thou marry me,
And thy first wife alive, then poison me,
To purchase my poor dower?

Chartley What shall I say, or think, or do? I am at a nonplus.

Gratiana Hast thou the face, thou brazen impudence,
To look upon me past grace?

Chartley Thou canst not properly call me past grace, for I never enjoyed thee yet. I cannot tell whether I blush or no, but I have now at this time, more grace than I can tell what to do with.

Gratiana Who drew thee to this folly?

Chartley Who but the old dotard, thy father, who when I was honestly married to a civil maid, he persuaded me to leave her. I was loath at first, but after entreating, urging, and offering me large proffers, I must confess I was seduced to come a-wooing to thee.

Gratiana My father, villain?

Chartley Aye, thy father, Grace. And were he here I would justify it to the old dotard's face.

Sir Harry [*advancing*] Vile boy! Thou dar'st not be so impudent!
When did I meet thee, seek or sue to thee?
When? Name the day, the month, the hour, the year.

Chartley Plots, plots. I can but cry you mercy both.
Say that I have done you wrong, I can be but sorry for it. But indeed, to clear you, and lay the fault where it ought to be, all this comes from mine own father in the country, who hearing I had married with Luce, sends me word of his blessing to be divorced from her, and to come a suitor to your daughter.
I think you have his hand and seal to show.

Old Chartley [*advancing*] My hand and seal! When was that letter writ?

Chartley Heyday!
If you get one word more of me tonight,
But scurvy looks, I'll give you leave to hang me.

Sir Harry Vile boy!

Old Chartley Ungracious villain!

Gratiana Treacherous youth!

Sir Harry No grace at all?

Chartley No grace.

Old Chartley This is bad company who hath seduced thee. Speak, on my blessing, who hath thus misled thee? But no more lies, I charge thee.

Chartley Bad company hath been the shame of me. I was as virtuously given as any youth in Europe, till I fell into one Boyster's company. 'Tis he that hath done all the harm upon me.

Boyster [*aside*] I?

Chartley And if he should deny it?

Boyster [*advancing*] What then? You'd cry him mercy.

Chartley I had best bite out my tongue and speak no more. What shall I do, or what shall I say? There is no outfacing them all. Gentlemen, fathers, wives, or what else, I have wronged you all. I confess it that I have; what would you more? Will any of you rail of me? I'll bear it. Will any of you beat me? So they strike not too hard, I'll suffer it. Will any of you challenge me? I'll answer it. What would you have me say or do? One of these I have married, the other I have betrothed, yet both maids for me. Will you have me take one, and leave the t'other? I will. Will you have me keep them both? I will.

Luce's father [*advancing*] Perjured, not mine.

Chartley What, you here too? Nay then, I see all my good

friends are met together. Wilt thou have me, Luce? I am thy husband, and had I not loved thee better than Grace, I had not disappointed the marriage day tomorrow.

Luce Lascivious, no.

Chartley Wilt thou have me Grace, for had I not loved thee better than Luce, I would never after I had married her been contracted to thee.

Gratiana Inconstant, no.

Chartley Then neither married man, widower nor bachelor. What's to be done? Here's even the proverb verified, "between two stools, the tail goes to ground".

Sir Harry Now I bethink me this our meeting here
Is wondrous strange. Call in the gentlewoman
That owns this house.

Enter SENCER *like a gentleman and the* WISE WOMAN

Boyster Old trot, I'll trounce thee. Here is the marriage proved 'twixt Luce and Chartley. Witch, this was not your promise.

Wise Woman Have patience, and in the end we'll pay you all. Your worships are most heartily welcome. I made bold to send for you, and you may see to what end, which was to discover unto you the wild vagaries of this wanton wag-pasty, a wild-oats, I warrant him. And, Sir Harry, that your daughter hath scaped this scouring, thank this gentleman, and then make of him as he deserves.

Sir Harry Oh, I remember him.

Gratiana He never pleas'd mine eye so well as now.
I know his love, and he in Chartley's place
My favour shall possess.

Sencer Thanks, my sweet Grace.

Sir Harry Aye, and the more th'inconstant youth to spite,
Sencer, I give her thee in Chartley's sight.

Chartley There's one gone already, but this is my wife and her I'll keep in spite both of the devil and his dam.

Wise Woman Not from her lawful husband.

Chartley That am I.

Wise Woman That is the gentleman [*pointing to* BOYSTER].
Accept him, Luce;
And you, the like of her. Nay, I'll make it good:
This gentleman married you vizarded, you him disguised, mistaking him for Chartley, which none but my boy Jack was privy to. After, she changed her habit with him, as you with Jack. And you in Mistress Luce's habit –

Luce May I believe you, mother?

Wise Woman This be your token.

Boyster Her that I married, I wrung twice by the finger.

Luce Of that token my hand was sensible.

Boyster And ere the clamorous and loud noise begun,
I whispered to her thus. [*Whispers to* LUCE]

Luce You are the man.

Boyster Thanks, grannam. What thou promis'd, thou hast done.

Luce's father And leaving him, I take you for my son.

Chartley Two gone, then where's the third? This makes me mad.
Where is my wife, then? For a wife I had.

Wise Woman Not see thy wife? Come hither, Jack, my boy.
Nay take him to thee and with him all joy.

Old Chartley Well art thou served to be a general scorn
To all thy blood; and if not for our sakes,
For thy soul's health and credit of the world,
Have some regard to me, to me thy father.

Chartley Enough, sir. If I should say I would become a new
man, you would not take my word.
If I should swear, I would amend my life,
You would not take mine oath. If I should bind
Myself to become an honest man, you would
Scarce take my bond.

Old Chartley I should do none of these.

Chartley Then see, sir, when to all your judgements I see me past grace, do I lay hold of grace, and here begin to retire myself. This woman hath lent me a glass, in which I see all my imperfections, at which my conscience doth more blush inwardly than my face outwardly. And now I dare confidently undertake for myself I am honest.

Luce 2 Then I dare confidently undertake to help you to a wife who desires to have an honest man or none. Look on me well; simple though I stand here, I am your wife. Blush not at your folly, man, perhaps I have more in me than you expect from me.

Chartley Knavery and riot, both which are now to me mean

forage. [*Searching her*]

Luce 2 You and I have been better acquainted,
And yet search me not too far least you shame me.
Look on me well; nay better, better yet.
I'll assure you I left off a petticoat
When I put on these breeches. What say you now?
Scattering her ha

Chartley First love and best beloved?

Luce 2 Let me be both or neither.

Wise Woman [*aside*] My boy turned girl? I hope she'll keep my counsel. From henceforth, I'll never entertain any servant but I'll have her searched.

Old Chartley Her love hath drawn her hither after him. –
My loving daughter, welcome. Thou hast run
A happy course to see my son thus chang'd.

Chartley Father, call me once again your son, and Sir
Harry, me your friend. Sencer, an hand; and
Mistress Grace, an heart in honourable love.
Where I have wronged you Luce, forgive. Impute
My errors to my youth, not me. With Grace
I interchange an embrace; with you, Luce,
A parting buss. I wish you all joy;
Divide my heart amongst you, [*to* LUCE 2] thou, my soul.
Nay, mother midnight, there's some love for you.
Out of thy folly, being reputed wise,
We, self-conceited, have our follies found.
Bear thou the name of all these comic acts.
Luce, Luce, and Grace – Oh, covetous man! I see
I sought to engross what now sufficeth three,
Yet each one wife enough. One nuptial feast

Shall serve three bridals, where be thou chief guest!

Exeunt all

FINIS

COMMENDATORY VERSE

To his chosen Friend
the learned Author Mr Thomas Heywood

Thou wants no herald to divulge thy fame;
'T needs no apology. Only thy name
Into judicious readers doth infuse
A will to add a laurel to thy muse.
Was now *Mæcænas* living, how would he
Support thy learned wit, whose industry
Hath purchas'd such a knowing skill, that those
Who read, admire thee, lest some critic shows
His ignorance in seeking with new songs
To gain the honour which to thee belongs.
But let pale envy belch forth all her spite
Thy candid fame shall still continue white,
Unspotted, pure, and fair, till memory
Be turn'd oblivion, or a deity
Prove mortal. And when *Atropos* shall do
The fatal office her belongs unto;
Apollo will rebreathe a life in thee
In length to equal all eternity,
Where in Elysian joys he will so raise
Thy worth where never wither shall the bays
Wherewith he crowns thee. So thy works will show
The debt I pay's no more but what I owe.

Samuel King

Glossarial Notes

Dramatis Personae

1 ROBIN Young Chartley's first name is mentioned only once at 1.2.166, when he rehearses his marriage vows. The name has strong folkloric and literary connotations. In the sixteenth and seventeenth centuries, Robin Goodfellow was believed to be a capricious, mischievous goblin who haunted the English country-side. Also referred to as Hobgoblin or Puck, Robin Goodfellow's most popular incarnation is as a dramatic character in Shakespeare's *A Midsummer Night's Dream*. Suggestively, Heywood hints at Robin Goodfellow again at 2.2.221, soon after an allusion to Shakespeare's play at 2.2.214-5.

3 BOYSTER from the adjective 'boistous', whose later variants 'boisteous' or 'boystuous' led to the modern 'boisterous'. When referred to a person, 'boistous' meant rough, coarse and unpolished.

GRATIANA full of grace – this sense is the source of numerous puns in Act 5. See, for example, 'past grace' at 5.2.111 and 5.2.235, to have 'more grace' at 5.2.114-5, or to 'lay hold of grace' at 5.2.235. But also gracious – as suggested by the location of Sir Harry's household in Gracious Street, i.e. Gracechurch Street.

5 SENCER from the verb to censure, to give an opinion or to find fault with, blame, condemn; an appropriate name for Sir Boniface's unrelenting opponent in the amusing contest at the beginning of Act 4.

TABOR a small kind of drum, used chiefly as an accompaniment to the pipe or trumpet. Hence the puns at 2.2.27 and 2.2.120. See, Beaumont and Fletcher, *The Knight of the Burning Pestle*: 'March out … to Hogsdon … Up then I say, both young and old, both man and maid a Maying,/ With Drums and Guns that bounce aloud, and merry Taber playing' (4.1.447-51).

6 *conceited* witty

9 HOXTON Alternatively spelt 'Hogsdon' until the first half of the eighteenth century ('Hogsdon' or 'Hogsden' in Q), Hoxton, which was described by Stowe as 'a large street with houses on both sides', became a notorious place of entertainment and recreation in the early seventeenth century. See, Marston's *The Scourge of Villanie: Three Books of Satyres*: 'At Hogsdon now his monstrous lust he feasts,/ For there he keeps a bawdy-house of beasts.' (3.41); Jonson' *The Alchemist*: 'Gallants, men, and women,/ And of all sorts, tag-rag, been seen to flock here/ In threaves, these ten weeks, as to a second Hogsden/ In days of Pimlico and Eye-bright' (5.2.17-20); or Fletcher and Beaumont's *The Knight of the Burning Pestle*: 'March ou and shew your willing minds, by twenty, and by twenty,/ To Hogsdon or to Newington, where Ale and Cakes are plenty.' (4.1.446-7) Ben Jonson refers to a witch who dwelt 'about Kentish Town or Hogsdon' in his comedy *The Devil is an Ass*.

16 LUCE 2 Not in the original list of *Dramatis Personae*. The implications of Heywood's decision to give two of his main female characters in this play the same name are discussed in the Introduction, p. xiii-xiv.

1.1

2 *cast* a throw of dice

6 *saying* right to speak

10 *except* object, take exception

16 *beaver* a hat made of the fur of the beaver, worn chiefly by men; see also 3.3.187

26 *set* stake, wager

27 *set in gold* the ring Chartley mentions at 1.1.29
29 *bale* set, pair
31 *Hold me play* keep me engaged
32 *take … order* take measures or steps
34 *more* again
40 *set you* formulaic expression used to announce that the bets are placed and that the players have agreed to roll the dice
41 *at all* exclamation accompanying each throw
43 *Gramercy* mercy on us, from old French, *grant merci*
cinques throws of the dice that turn up five
49 *this at the candlestick* Dave Golz has kindly pointed out to me that although Heywood's use of this phrase may suggest a technical term for the throwing or flinging of dice, there are no other recorded occurences in contemporary drama. Candlesticks, however, are common in gaming scenes, because they are part of the furnishings of ordinaries and dicing houses (private correspondence).
50 *Todo* all (Spanish)
52 *via* go (Italian)
54 *treys* throws of the dice that turn up three
55 *old dog* adept
57 *Be my half one cast* give me half of my wager; see also 1.1.59
59 *will be my half?* see 1.1.57
60 *frank* liberal, lavish in dealing with money; see Etherege, *Man of Mode* (5.1): 'Lose it all like a frank gamester on the square'
62 *cross* a coin bearing the figure of a cross; see word play at lines 63 and 64, where 'cross' stands for a religious emblem
82 *pox of* exclamation of irritation or impatience, followed either by the preposition 'of' (see Shakespeare's *Love's Labour's Lost*, 'A pox of that jest' 5.2.46) or by the now more common preposition 'on' (see Shakespeare's *All's Well That Ends Well*, 'A pox on him' 4.3.307).
89 *rapiers* swords
92 *you … play* possible metadramatic reference to 'playing', i.e. 'acting', as well as 'gambling'; the topical debate on the 'purpose of playing'

produced famous apologies, including Sir Philip Sidney's *The Defence of Poesie* (1595) and Thomas Heywood's *An Apology for Actors* (1612), and notorious attacks, including Stephen Gosson's *Playes Confuted in Five Actions* (1582) and Philip Stubbes's *The Anatomie of Abuses* (1583).

97 *chafing* excitement, vexation

99 *testy* headstrong

waspish irritable

103-4 *give good counsel … take it* proverbial (Tilley C100)

111 *Gracious Street* Gracechurch Street; Stow describes it as being lined with 'many fair houses for merchants and artificers, and many fair inns for travellers (Stow, 157). The 'fair inns' in Gracechurch Street included the Bell, whose innyard was used for playing by leading companies, such as the Queen's Men in the 1580s. Also known as 'Grasschurch Street', because of the 'herb-market there kept' (Stow, 191). See also *Dramatis Personae* 3.

touched you guessed your meaning, but also hurt your feelings, as Sencer makes clear in the next line

125 *lightly* without the money and goods they have lost

127 *somewhat* something

130 *proclamations* declarations

139 *dandiprat* a small sixteenth-century coin, worth three and a half pence; hence petit, small-sized. Also, a character in Dekker/Middleton's *Blurt, Master Constable* (1602).

147 *stands … light* undermines her own chances; proverbial (Tilley L276)

149 *gyves* fetters

155 *ordinary* public house; the term was often used as synonymous with 'gambling-house', because the more expensive ordinaries were frequented by men of fashion, and dinner was usually followed by gambling; see also 5.1.9

156 *the Exchange* the Old Royal Exchange on Cornhill, described by Stow in his *Survey of London* (1598) as 'a burse, or place for

merchants to assemble' (173); see also 3.3.211
158 *solicit* try to win her favour

1.2

1-3 *Where … little* curious ironic theological resonance playing on Joseph's name and the topography of heaven and earth
7 *ply* to devote oneself to
11 *awe* power to inspire fear or reverence
12 *overseer* supervisor
26 *intend* attend to
28 *flout* mock
50 *poles* the North and the South Poles
57 *a bone to gnaw upon* proverbial (Tilley B516)
66 *angels* gold coins bearing the image of the archangel Michael; see also 4.1.158 and 4.3.41
71 *reverence* regard with reverence
79 *fig* not to care or to give a fig, meaning not to care at all. See, for example, Shakespeare's *Othello*, where Iago remarks: 'Virtue? a fig!' (1.3.319) and 'Blest fig's-end!' (2.1.249). Also bawdy, in expressions of contempt, often accompanied by a rude gesture, in which the thumb is thrust between the index and middle fingers. Patridge (112) suggests that the English expression follows closely the French *foutre* and the Italian *fico* or *fica*. Used by several Jacobean dramatists, including Shakespeare. See Pistol's lines in *2 Henry IV* – 'When Pistol lies, do this; and fig me, like the bragging Spaniard' (5.3.117-18) – and in *Henry V* – 'Die and be damn'd; and figo for thy friendship!' (3.6.58) and 'The fig of Spain!' (3.6.60).
89 *stock* source, origin, kind, but also the goods referred to at line 1.1.156-7 and a bawdy allusion to the male organ, the fruits of Chartley's love for Luce being their offspring.

93-6 *Honour … worshipful* echoes of Falstaff's famous speech in Shakespeare's *1 Henry IV*: 'What is honour? A word. What is in that word honour? What is that honour? Air.' (5.1.134-5)

96 *right worshipful* honorific title and form of address; see also 4.1.7

115 *jackanapes* tame monkey

116 *Dædalus* the mythological builder of the labyrinth, inhabited by the Minotaur, the bull-headed monster slain by Theseus. The latter found his way in and out of the labyrinth thanks to Ariadne, who furnished him with a wondrous thread. See also 4.1.152

119 *last* wooden model of the foot, on which shoemakers stretched their leather to make shoes and boots; this image suggests that Chartley might be alluding to his desire to possess Luce sexually.

121 *stomach* gastronomic (and sexual) appetite; see also 1.2.153

124 *know not the way* .. bawdy allusion, as made clear by lines 127-28

132 *earnest* pun on Luce's commitment and the small sum of money usually paid to secure a bargain; see also 4.1.170 and 4.1.209

142 *motion* proposal; see also 2.2.219 and 5.1.77

147 *see* deem fit, proper

148 *take order* see 1.1.32

149 *Stay* wait

152 *diet* food

153 *stomach* see 1.2.121

156 *lay them up* put them away for safety

158 *night-cap* a covering for the head, normally worn in bed; hence a sign of a settled and respectable life-style. See, for example, Shakespeare's *Othello* (2.1.302), where Iago vents his suspicions about Cassio's affair with his wife: 'For I fear Cassio with my night-cap too'.

164 *thereby hangs a tale* … there is something to tell about that; proverbial (Tilley T48)

173 *conceit* idea

178 *a-days* by day

to bring wholly, thoroughly (Verity 263)

179 *a-nights* by night
whiting-mop young whiting or gurnard, i.e. a small fish
190 *exploit* feat, act of extreme courage or skill; clearly ironic
193 *beldam* hag, old woman; see also 2.1.112 and 4.3.54
195 *anon* at once
196 *punctually* precisely, accurately
197 *Sir John* derogative for priest
201 *light of* learn
206 *fantastic* capricious
213 *aims* plans (to marry in secret)

2.1

1 *moil* drudgery
7 *water* urine; see also Shakespeare's *Twelfth Night*, 'Carry his water to th' wise woman' (3.4.103) and *2 Henry IV*, 'Sirrah, you giant, what says the doctor to my water?' (1.2.1)
8 *limbeck* alembic, still, i.e. her bladder
12 *hit* guessed; see also 4.3.18-9
21-2 *see as far into a millstone* be acute, perceptive; proverbial (Tilley, M 965)
24 *casting of waters* analysis of a client's urine
24-5 *Mother Bomby* the title character in a comedy written by John Lyly (1594); see also 4.4.88
25-6 *Pepper Alley* located off Long Southwark (now Southwark Bridge Road), near a leather market (Stow, 365)
27 *Coldharbour* a mayoral house, 'with all tenements and key adjoining' in Dowgate Ward, between St. Paul's and London Bridge (Stow, 211-2)
28 *Golden Lane* near Hoxton (Stow, 378)
29 *forespeaking* predictions, prophecies; see also 3.1.167
33 *'recting a figure* casting horoscopes

34-5 *the book and the key* more commonly, “key and book”, “the book” standing for the Bible; tools used in a method of divination

35 *sieve … shears* well-know practice; see Ben Jonson’s *The Alchemist*: ‘have all thy tricks/ Of coz’ning with a hollow cole, dust, scrapings,/ Searching for things lost, with a sieve and shears, …’ (1.1.93-5)

40 *trot* old woman; see also 3.1.102, 4.3.63 and 5.2.185

60 *presently* at once

67 *by my truly* by my troth; in truth

74 *Kent Street* in the Borough of Southwark, renown for the Loke, a lazar house

78 *wag* joker, wit

84 *Ptolemy* astronomer, mathematician and geographer (ca 87-150 AD). According to his geocentric theory, commonly referred to as the “Ptolemaic System”, the sun and the other planets in the solar system orbited the earth.

84-5 *Erra Pater* a mythological astrologer

86 *presently* see line 2.1.60

92 *fidelity* word of honour

97 *stripling* young lad, youth

99 *Statute of Winchester* famous statute passed by Edward I in 1285; another anachronistic reference, this time to the reign of Edward II and his descendants, occurs at 4.2.115. This might also be an oblique reference to the fact that the Bishop of Winchester owned the land on which the Bankside brothels stood.

102-3 *I shall want … have* bawdy reminder of Luce’s sexual identity

107 *Mother Redcap’s* a famous tavern in Camden Town owned by a notorious sorceress; what Heywood refers to here, however, is more likely to be another tavern with the same sign in Holloway Road, between Hoxton and Lower Highbury; see also 4.3.6-7

112 *beldam* see 1.2.193

116 *wild oats* youthful follies, excesses; see also 5.2.192

118 *Hecate* goddess of the crossroads, often wrongly associated, as here, with witchcraft, black magic and evil

Proserpine goddess of the underworld

119 *conjuring up spirits* excite sexually, although at 2.1.122, and then again at 2.1.163-4, the Wise Woman interprets similar remarks literally, meaning 'invoking the spirits of the dead', which was regarded as black magic and hence prosecuted as a devilish practice. The Wise Woman's anxiety has a topical ring, as Henry VIII's Statute of 1541 prohibiting sorcery was confirmed in 1604 and James I's tract *Of Daemonologie*, which was first published in Edinburgh in 1597, was re-published in London in 1603.

128 *dromedary* possibly a reference the Wise Woman's hunched back

129 *racket* loud noise, uproar

129-30 *she-caterwaulers* cats in heat making noise; hence, the prostitutes hired by the Wise Woman

137 *mere* downright, absolute

141 *turnbroach* turnspit

142 *Jack* typical name for the ordinary man, for a representative of the common people

144 *cutting Dick* swaggering bully; Dick Evans was a notorious highwayman whose name had become proverbial by 1600. Heywood received one pound on 30th September 1603 for revising an anonymous play called *Cutting Dick*. Both the anonymous play and Heywood's revised version are now lost.

150 *daughter* this term suggests familiarity rather than any degree of actual kinship between Luce and the Wise Woman; the affectionate quality of the Wise Woman's reference to Luce highlights the incongruity between Luce's apparently virtuous and upright nature and her disconcerting familiarity with the Wise Woman and her associates. Luce's ambiguous relation to the Wise Woman is brought up again at 2.1.177-8, when the Wise Woman refers to Luce as 'one of my daughters'.

smug pretty, smooth

152 *bespoke* engaged, asked

161 *wise .. words* proverbal (Tilley W 781)

162 *I am … I am* Biblical allusion. See *Exodus* 3.13-14: 'And Moses said unto God, Behold, when I come unto the children of Israel, and shall say unto them, The God of your fathers hath sent me unto you; and they shall say to me, What is his name? What shall I say unto them? And God said unto Moses, I am that I am, and he said, Thus shalt thou say unto the children of Israel, I am hath sent me unto you.' See also Shakespeare's *Othello*, where Iago says: 'I am not what I am' (1.1.65). In Shakespeare, the Biblical echo is used to stress the villain's blasphemous positioning of himself as the opposite of anything godly and good.
there's an end this shall be the end

163-4 *Can'st … word!* see note at 2.1.119

174 *complexion* physical constitution, the combination of the four humours, which were believed to determine the nature of the body

176 *grannam* grandmother, old woman

177 *As well …dish* proverbial (Tilley, 234)

177-8 *she … daughters* see note at 2.1.150

179 *pieces* English gold coins

183 *betimes* early, in the morning; speedily

184 *grannam* see 2.1.176

185 *hedge-stakes* stout sticks to form component parts of a fence or hedge

191 *'tired* attired, dressed

202-3 *warrant* the repetition of this verb anticipates the comic resolution

2.2

5 *sad* serious

11 *unthrift* dissolute, profligate person; see also 2.2.55

16 *quarter's wages* three months' salary; see also 2.2.41

22-3 *nick* critical moment, *in flagrante delicto*; also bawdy allusion to female genitalia, from 'nick' as 'wound', 'slit'

24 *highway* another bawdy allusion to female genitalia, suggesting sexual promiscuity
27 *pipe* windpipe; a pun on Tabor's name (see also 2.2.120 and '*Dramatis Personae*' line 5)
29 *full butt* head-on, full tilt; allusion to sexual intercourse
34 *Be with you* God be with you
41 *quarter's wages* see 2.2.16
52 *my daughter's young* Sir Harry's argument echoes Capulet's in Shakespeare's *Romeo and Juliet*. When Paris asks for Juliet's hand, Capulet replies: 'My child is yet a stranger in the world,/ She hath not seen the change of fourteen years./ Let two more summers wither in their pride/ Ere we may think her ripe to be a bride.' Both Sir Harry and Capulet change their mind when interests far greater than their daughters' welfare are at stake.
55 *unthrifts* see 2.2.11
58 *counter* the prison attached to a city court
66 *Mitre* the sign of two famous London taverns; the reference here is more likely to be to the Mitre in Bread Street, Cheapside, rather than the Mitre in Fleet Street (Sugden, 348)
68 *fast* fast asleep
78 *for love … money* proverbial (Tilley L484)
80 *souse* heavy blow
84 *without control* unrestrainedly, freely, hence ironic, as he is in jail
104 *ere* before
tasted tested
117 *ere* see 2.2.104
120 *tabor* pun on Tabor's name. See 2.2.27 and '*Dramatis Personae*', line 5.
131 *yclept* called
132-3 *to give … Jack Drum's Entertainment* to turn out of doors; the title of a comedy acted by the Children of Paul's, which was entered in the Stationers' Register in September 1600 and printed soon after
134 *play upon* play the drum, or tabor (see '*Dramatis Personae*', line 5);

also take advantage of. This line, when read alongside Tabor's reference to his 'pipe' at 2.2.27, echoes Shakespeare's *Hamlet*, 3.2.355-61: 'You would play upon me, you would seem to know my stops, you would pluck out the heart of my mystery, you would sound me from my lowest note to the top of my compass; and there is much music, excellent voice, in this little organ, yet cannot you make it speak. 'Sblood, do you think I am easier to be played on than a pipe?'

135 *hare* prostitute, from its close assonance with 'hoar'/'whore'; see Mercutio's lines in Shakespeare's *Romeo and Juliet*, 2.3.132-7: 'An old hare hoar,/ And an old hare hoar,/ Is very good meat in Lent./ But a hare that is hoar/ Is too much for a score/ When it hoars ere it be spent.'

145-6 *A cat … king* proverbial (Tilley, C141)

159 *played them away* accompanied them with instrumental music; showed them the way out

164-5 *Eques … virgo* 'Hail, worshipful knight; I greet you. I cannot see what[who]'s behind, but, virtuous maid, I bid you a good morrow'.

172 *Sit …omen* 'Be it a sign of good luck to you'; 'good luck to you'

175 *ere* see 2.2.104

178 *Intende … nobilis* 'Pay attention, noble sir'; 'Listen carefully'

182 *Sir Henry* this reference to Sir Harry as Sir Henry characterizes Sir Boniface and his stuffiness

183 *preceptor … negligitis* 'The mentor teaches, [but] you neglect the truth'; 'you're not paying enough attention'.

185 *nidgets* fools

191 *Vir bone* good man

192 *bones* trouble, problems

201 *Mille … modis* in thousands of ways

212 *dispatched* dealt with

214 *Familist* a member of the family; also a member of 'The Family of Love', a religious sect strongly influenced by radical reformers. It started in continental Europe around 1540 and then flourished in

England in the sixteenth and seventeenth centuries. Tabor's reference to Sir Boniface as a 'Familist' represents a comic inversion of the familist belief in salvation through the pursuit of unity and perfect love with God.

214-5 *I shall … acquaintance* an echo from Shakespeare's *A Midsummer Night's Dream*, where Bottom expresses a similar wish, 'I shall desire you of more acquaintance' three times, while addressing Cobweb, Peaseblossom and Mustardseed at 3.1.175-88; see also *Dramatis Personae* 1 and 2.2.221

216 *physiognomy* the art of judging character from bodily features; the comic sense of Tabor's remark becomes clear at 2.2.232

218 *Quomodo … vales* goodbye, farewell

219 *motion* see 1.2.142

220 *out of doors* to be sent out, presumably on a fictitious errand

221 *good fellow* a possible allusion to Puck, or Robin Goodfellow, a character in Shakespeare's *A Midsummer Night's Dream*, especially in light of the earlier echo from the same play at line 2.2.214-5; see also *Dramatis Personae* 1

223 *Vale … magno* farewell, great man

224 *Saint Magnus* Saint Magnus Church, at the north end of London Bridge

225-8 *Gracious Street* see 1.1.111 and *Dramatis Personae* 3

226-7 *virgo … valete* goodbye, fair virgin and goodbye, charming master

3.1

11 *colour* pretence; see also 4.4.77

13 *with a wet finger* easily

25 *clap* generally venereal disease, but here, more specifically copulation, from the verb 'to clap', 'to strike together'

32 *gossips* godparents

39-40 *string … bow* proverbial (Tilley S937)

44 *free of* have the freedom to perform; the liberty, or right, to trade
45 *charter* licence
46 *make* describe, represent, regard
49 *tell* count
68 *mystery* craft, art, profession; a pun on the Wise Woman's tricks
74 *but* only
76 *against* before
78 *Sit … quies* 'A good day, good health and peace be with you'
81 *conjunction* a pun on wedding or union and all the inflectional forms belonging to a verb
85 *he … he* Chartley
90 SD *vizard* mask
94 *hoodwinked* covered up from sight, disguised; but also, in the modern sense, Chartley is being tricked, deceived.
102 *Gramercy* see 1.1.43
trot see 2.1.40
111 *grannam* see 2.1.176
116 *Pocas palabras* few words (Spanish)
119 *stay* marry
122 *quittance* retaliation, reprisal
137 *warrants* protectors
pursuivants junior officers attached to a nobleman; presumably in charge of finding the lady
138 SD *affrighted* frightened
141 *Curro … cucurri* three inflected forms of the verb 'to run'
142 *murrey* purple red
151 *prove to* speed
167 *forespeaking* see 2.1.29
169 *gentlewomen lodgers* prostitutes; see Mistress Quickly in Shakespeare's *King Henry V*, 2.1.32-5: ' … we cannot lodge and board a dozen or fourteen gentlewomen that live honestly by the prick of their needles, but it will be thought we keep a bawdy-house straight.'

3.2

6 *Hob-man blind* blind man's buff; see one of its variant forms in *Hamlet*: 'What devil was't/ That thus hath cozen'd you at hoodman-blind?' (3.4.76-7)

7 *in tenebris* in the dark

8 *grannam* the Wise Woman; see 2.1.176

8-9 *younger brother* a match with a 'broken commodity' (i.e. a "spoiled" virgin) would result in Boyster being disinherited, or becoming 'a younger brother'

12 *grannam* see 3.2.8 and 2.1.176

15 *ere* see 2.2.104

17 *hobbledehoy* clumsy youth

23 *woe* woeful

26 *like* likely

28 *cracked ware* see also 'broken commodity' at 3.2.10

31 *set … fire* a possible allusion to the Gunpowder Plot; see also 3.2.40 and 5.2.129

bobbed cheated; but also, to move up and down, hence bawdy; see also 3.2.32

40 *gunpowder … witch* a possible allusion to the Gunpowder Plot (1605). It is suggestive that the Catholic Lord Monteagle, who passed on a warning letter to Cecil, had a house in Hoxton. Other allusions occur at 3.2.31 and 5.2.129. For more details, see Editor's Introduction, pp. xi-xii.

41 *fitters* very small pieces, shreds

42 *put up* literally, sheathe one's sword, therefore 'forbear', 'hold back'

43 *jeer* object of mockery

3.3

39 *cognizance* acquaintance

51 *captious* misleading, obscure

60 *shittle* inconstant, fickle

61 *a-wool-gathering* indulgent thoughts and fantasies

64 *coxcomb* fool, simpleton; see also 3.3.220 and 4.1.217

67 *choke-pear* hard and coarse variety

68 *popering* delicious variety of pears imported from Poperingues in Flanders

71 *make away* normally followed by 'with', meaning to 'kill'

72 *compass her* succeed in obtaining her ('her' refers to Gratiana)

73 *outface* contradict defiantly

80 *cope … away* exchange, barter

94 *ere* see 2.2.104

102 *betimes* early, speedily

113 *an humble* the spelling of the indefinite article reflects a contemporary weak articulation of the initial *h* (Kökeritz, 308); see also 5.1.34 and 5.2.262-3

120 *broker to lewd lust* pander, go-between, procurer; see also 4.4.59

158-9 *Woman Killed with Kindness* popular domestic tragedy written by Heywood (see Editor's Introduction, p. xi), aptly mentioned here as Chartley suggests that Luce and her father might waste away with sadness, like Anne Frankford in Heywood's popular play. Another reference to the play occurs at 3.3.169-70, as Chartley's pledge would remind Heywood's audience of the seeming kindness and generosity with which Master Frankford provides for his unfaithful wife.

166 *quarter* three months; see 2.2.16 and 2.2.41

174 *Gramercy* see 1.1.43

178 *Bristol stone* rock-crystal from Bristol, better known as the "Bristol diamond"

180 *stones* precious stones, but also testicles

181 *right* authentic, genuine

184 *lay up* put by, save
186 *branched* embroidered
187 *wrought* decorated
beaver see 1.1.16
191 *Gramercy* see 1.1.43
192 *ere* see 2.2.104
211 *Cheapside* central area in the City of London between St. Paul's and the Exchange, which took its name from a market held in the large street of West Cheaping
Exchange see 1.1.156
220 *Coxcomb* see 3.3.64
221 *rattle-baby* frivolous, foolish person
222 *go to buffets* fight, scuffle
223 *cuff* strike
227 *Deed* indeed

4.1

3 *limit* appoint
7 *right worshipful* Sir Harry; see also 1.2.96
23 *cashiered* dismissed
26-7 *Venerabiles … capistri* 'venerable instructors, never be muzzled'
28-9 *Et … salve* 'And, once again, good morrow, master bald-head'
30 *Amo … amavi* paradigm of the verb 'to love'.
33-4 *tongue-men* people who have the gift to speak in languages unknown to them; normally associated with worship and mystic possession
35 *budgets* wallets
41 *Nec …utroque* 'Neither in spirit, nor in [our] hearts; no way'
46 *Domine … rogas?* 'Master, why do you ask?'
51 *Brasenose* college in Oxford; the joke at line 52 is made more explicit by the original spelling, 'Brazen nose'
54 *Petrus dormit securus* Peter sleeps untroubled

Peterhouse college in Cambridge, probably attended by Heywood himself. In the prefatory matter to the 1658 edition of Heywood's 'An Apology for Actors', William Cartwright claims that Heywood was a fellow of Peterhouse. Dr Pattenden (Senior Tutor at Peterhouse) has kindly drawn my attention to an entry in the *Peterhouse Biographical Register* (259), according to which 'we may unhesitatingly dismiss his claim to a Fellowship (which may have arisen out of some later confusion: *Ralph Heywood* was Fellow in 1650), [although] membership is strongly supported by passages from his own pen' (private correspondence). On such assumption F.G.Fleay argues that Heywood might have acted Sencer himself. See also Editor's Introduction, p. xiv.

55 *Natus eram* I was born

Woxford possibly Wixford in Warwickshire, or Yoxford in Suffolk, or perhaps made up for the sake of the rhyme (E.H.Sugden, 572)

56-64 *Est … papaver* the Latin phrases which Sencer uses in this speech have a merely aural function, as they sound similar to the bogus translation Sencer provides for Sir Harry's benefit.

57 *Gotham* proverbial place renowned for the folly of its inhabitants

59 *genes fustian* coarse Genoese cotton fabric, now widely used and currently referred to as 'jeans' or 'blue jeans'

61 *tee-hee* titter, giggle

67 *Nominativo … prediculus* another nonsensical Latin phrase, which rhymes with its supposed translation 'his words are most ridiculous

70 *construe* translate, expound

70-1 *Est … fines* 'There is measure in [all] things; there are indeed fixed limits'

72-3 *Est … fishes* Sencer gives the wrong translation, which, however, sounds like the Latin phrase, and therefore rings right to the ignorant Sir Harry. Shakespeare exploits the comic potential of mock translations of Latin *sententiae* in *The Taming of the Shrew*. See, for example, Lucentio, who uses Latin to distract Hortensio's attention, while addressing his mock translation to Bianca: '*Hic ibat*, as I told you before – *Simois*, I am Lucentio – *hic est*, son unto Vincentio of Pisa – *Sigeia tellus*, disguised thus to get your love – *Hic steterat*, and that Lucentio that comes a-wooing – *Priami*, is my man Tranio – *regia*, bearing my port – *celsa senis*, that we might beguile the old pantaloon' (3.1.31-6). Bianca herself provides a different mock translation, thus reinforcing the comic potential of this witty device: '*Hic ibat Simois*, I know you not – *hic est Sigeia tellus*, I trust you not – *Hic steterat Priami*, take heed he hear us not – *regia*, presume not – *celsa senis*, despair not. (3.1.40-43). See also 4.1.98

75 *Dii … boni* 'Dear sweet God'; an expression of exasperation

76 *bones* see 2.2.192

78-9 Καρτερε … σοφων These two Greek lines, like most of the Latin used by Sir Boniface and Sencer in this scene, are badly corrupt as they appear in the 1638 Quarto, possibly as a result of the compositor's lack of a classical education. Two scholars have suggested two slightly variant translations. The following translation was kindly provided by Richard Proudfoot: 'Steadfast poet, nursling and best beloved of the Muse,/ Eloquent expositor of logic, not least of the wise.' (Richard Proudfoot, private correspondence). The slightly variant alternative provided by Derek Hughes reads as follows: 'Mighty son of the Muses, much and most beloved friend of poetry,/ Public exponent of logic, [and] not the least of the wise.' (Derek Hughes, private correspondence) The only substantial difference between the two translations originates from the non-sensical 'poetatis' at 4.1.78, which the two scholars emend and therefore translate differently.

80 *materna lingua* mother tongue

83 *denique* lastly

89 *Di … dum* mock Latin paradigm

91 *numquam … possit?* 'How can this be?'; 'How is this possible?'

92 *posset* cordial drink

95-6 *amo … titubavi* examples of verbs belonging to the first conjuntion;

the last is meant as a direct challenge to Sir Boniface, the verb *titubare* meaning 'to be uncertain', 'dither'

98 *Sir Timothy* the name Sencer adopts while in disguise, as 4.1.223 and 4.1.236-7 make clear; see also Shakespeare's *The Taming of the Shrew*, where Lucentio disguises himself like a pedant in order to gain access to Bianca and woo her. For other parallels with Shakespeare's play see 4.1.72-3.

99 *Bene, bene* 'That's correct'

102 *Vos … testis* 'You are, as I can witness it'

104 *pestis* plague

107-8 *Per … insanus* 'By these hands of mine, man, you are mad'; more commonly 'by this hand', as a way of introducing a solemn oath

109-10 *quid … grammatica* 'what is grammar?'

111 *Grammatica … ars* 'grammar is an art'

115 *Cato* Roman statesman, writer and orator, who lived between 234 and 149 BC

115-6 *Si … dicunt* 'If God is reason, as the prophecies tell us'

117 *Di – cunt* see similar misunderstanding in Shakespeare's *Henry V* 3.4.50-3, originating from Alice's mispronunciation of the word 'gown' during Katherine's language lesson: 'Katherine: 'Comment appellez-vous le pied et la robe?' Alice: 'Le foot, madame; et le count.' Katherine: 'Le foot, et le count? O Seigneur Dieu! Ils sont les mots de son mauvais, corruptible, gros, et impudique'

quotha he says

120 *subaudi* from *subaudio, -ire*, to understand, to be patient

123 *Propria … maribus* 'which becomes men'

126 *Venerabilis … ebrius* 'Venerable sir, that man is drunk'

129-30 *But if … perfect* Sir Harry, who is reproaching Sir Boniface for using what sounds to him like bawdy, indecent language, mentions the 'French tongue' because the French were associated with shallow morals, loose customs and, as a result, venereal diseases. See also Shakespeare's *Measure for Measure*: 'First Gentleman: … I had as lief be a list of an English kersey, as be piled, as thou art pilled, for a

French velvet.' (1.2.31-3) and Lucio's reference to the 'French crown' at 1.2.48, meaning both a familiar coin and the 'French disease', i.e. syphilis.

135 *Tellus* earth

150 *Quid … Timothy* 'What are you saying, Master Timothy?'

152 *Minos* King of Crete; he refused to sacrifice a white bull to the gods, and as a punishment, Poseidon had his wife fall in love with the bull and give birth to the Minotaur. See also 1.2.116.

158 *brace of angels* see 1.2.66

165 *Opus … usus* 'One needs experience'

167 *smoke* cause to smoke, as a result of heavy beating or whipping; the unusual turn of phrase here might suggest a misreading on the part of the compositor, as the original might have read 'smiten' or 'smyten', alternative infinitive forms of the verb 'to smite'

169 *Nobiles valete* 'Farewell, noble men'

quiete peace

170 *earnest* see 1.2.132 and 4.1.209

177 *Lusty Juventus* an interlude by Robert Weaver 'describing the frailtie of youth', published in London in 1565; quite aptly used in relation to the rakish Chartley

183 *Desperation* recklessness arising from despair; in keeping with the reference to the morality play tradition to which the old interlude mentioned at 4.1.177 belongs, where characters were often allegories of vices and virtues

190 *incident* pertinent, belonging; see also 4.1.231

greensickness chlorosis, a type of anaemia which gives the sufferer a characteristically greenish complexion

198 *jointure* joint holding of property; see also 5.1.66

201 *to boot* besides, additionally

209 *earnest* see 1.2.132 and 4.1.170

210 *hand and heart* possibly a corruption of 'hand on heart', i.e. a firm vow; for a more complex, indirect connection see Shakespeare's *Hamlet*, 'The head is not more native to the heart,/ The hand more

instrumental to the mouth,/ Than is the throne of Denmark to thy father' (1.2.47-49).

217 *coxcomb* see 3.3.64

231 *incident* see 4.1.190

241 *vindicta* Latin for revenge; see Hieronimo's famous invocation, "*vindicta mihi*", in Thomas Kyd's *The Spanish Tragedy* (publ. 1592)

242 *gorest* offend, spur, stab

horn worn by a cuckold, i.e. Chartley, once Sencer has won Gratiana for himself

4.2

2 *swagger* quarrel, squabble; see Falstaff and Hostess Quickly's exchange in Shakespeare's *2 Henry IV*, and, especially, Falstaff's remarks on Pistol at 2.4.97-8: 'He'll not swagger with a Barbary hen, if her feathers turn back in any show of resistance.'

16 *chapmen* dealers, customers

24 *blackamoor* black African

30 *ere* see 2.2.104

36 *abi* go away (Latin)

48 *Gracious Street* see 1.1.111 and *Dramatis Personae* 3

60 *tell-truth* truthful person

67 *apace* quickly

68 *falling sickness* epilepsy; the adjective 'falling' prompts the bawdy innuendoes at 4.2.69-74

75 *t'other* the other (of two); see also 5.2.165

76 *outface* see 3.3.73

81 *If he* if it was he

108 *board* literally 'table'; hence, metonymically, 'feast'

115 *John-a-Gaunt* John of Gaunt (1340-99), duke of Lancaster, fourth son of Edward III. John of Gaunt served under his brother, Edward the Black Prince during the Hundred Years War, leading armies

both to Spain and France. For another anachronistic reference to a remote past, see 2.1.99. In Shakespeare's *1 Henry IV* Falstaff refers to John of Gaunt as a paragon of military prowess: 'Indeed, I am not John of Gaunt your grandfather, but yet no coward, Hal.' (2.2.64-5)

116 *wards* defensive postures in fencing
foins thrusts

117-8 *St. George's Fields … Tuttle, Finsbury* three popular duelling spots. In Shakespeare's *2 Henry IV* Master Shallow reminisces about a night of revelry he spent with Falstaff in St. George's Fields: 'O, Sir John, do you remember since we lay all night in the Windmill in Saint George's Field? … Ha, 'twas a merry night! (3.2.189-92).

120 *Or … or* either … or

123 *leap-frog* a vengeful reference to Chartley leaping over a woman (his daughter Luce) to another (Gratiana); the audience, unlike Luce's father, know that Chartley had already forsaken Luce 2 for Luce

126 *Stafford Law* idiomatic expression used to suggest that the offended party will take justice into his own hands and punish the culprit corporally

127 *ferret* find and drive out, as with a ferret

4.3

6-7 *Mother Redcap's* see 2.1.107

11 *somewhat* something

18-9 *hit* see 2.1.12

41 *twenty angels* see 1.2.66

54 *beldam* see 1.2.193

55 *An* if

56 *mumble* handle roughly

60 *Apply thou* defend yourself

63 *trot* see 2.1.40

grannam see 2.1.176
65 *end* reason of his rage, i.e. his marriage to Luce 2, whom he believe to be a boy
77 *Fiat* So be it

4.4

1-11 Compare the opening of 4.2 in Shakespare's *Romeo and Juliet*
5 *proface* from the Latin *proficere*, to do good, to be advantageous; used as an expression, 'Much good may it do you'
7 *Sabre* cavalry sword; the name might ironically hint at the fact that Tabor has been carving
26 *Adesdem* a corruption from the Latin verb, *adire*, 'to come or to go near'
27 *sine dole* without trickery
puntis te vole nonsensical phrase used for the sake of the rhyme
29 *Gramercy* see 1.1.43
34 *dissemble* pay false professions, play the hypocrite
35 *Beso … manos* I kiss [your] hands
36 *À … service* your servant
44-5 *lead … a measure* lead a dance, but also bawdy allusion to the male member at 4.4.46-7
49 *whestone* fine-grained stone for sharpening cutting tools, or, as here figuratively, someone's wit
51 *ingenies* wits, intellectual talents
57 *"Farewell …Timothy"* see 4.1.234-5
59 *Pandarus* a character in Chaucer's *Troilus & Criseyde* and Shakespeare's *Troilus and Cressida*; a go-between, as at line 3.3.120. Both Chaucer and Shakespeare's source for this character was Homer's *Iliad*.
60-1 *turned … heels* died; see also 5.2.100
67 *rifled* spoiled, stolen

71 *quondam* former(ly)
77 *colour* see 3.1.11
88 *too good to be true* proverbial, as in John Lyly's *Mother Bomby* (4.2.208); an explicit allusion to Lyly's comedy occurs at 2.1.24-5
90 *post* now, with speed; see also 4.4.130 and 5.2.88
112 *ride* unwitting allusion to Chartley's secret rendezvous
122 *brock* base fellow; literally, badger
123 *travail* travel, physical exertion (also implicitly sexual, as hinted in Sencer's aside at 4.4.124)
130 *post* see 4.4.90

5.1

3 *Cheap Cross* a landmark at Cheapside; it was first erected in 1290 by Edward I in memory of his recently deceased wife, Queen Elianor, and then removed in 1643 by the Puritans, because it was decorated with images of the Virgin Mary
9 *ordinaries* see 1.1.155
12 *Grace Church* or Grass Church, dedicated to St. Bennet, in Bridge Ward, on the corner between Gracechurch Street and Lombard Street; see also 1.1.111 and *Dramatis Personae* 3
13 *bootless* useless, vain
24 *at six and at seven* phrase originally based on the language of dicing, denoting the hazard of one's whole fortune, and, in later use, as here, a failure to remove confusion, disorder or disagreement
30 *baulk* shun
34 *an heart* see 3.3.113
45 *This seven years day* time expression, commonly found in contemporary witness depositions, meaning 'during the past seven years to this day' (Jonathan Hope, private correspondence)
50 *clause* part
59 *take me with you* let me understand

66 *jointure* see 4.1.198
69 *approve* corroborate, confirm
77 *motion* see 1.2.142
78 *spleen* irritation
83 *jack* cunning, crafty fellow
88 *hereon* on this matter

5.2

2 *Presume* assume confidently
5 *Grannam* see 2.1.176
6 *hole* secret place where unlawful occupations are pursued; also, the orifice of any organ or part of the body, especially the mouth, the anus or female genitalia.
11 *several rooms* The Victorian editor A. W. Verity helped his readers imagine Chartley's victims overlooking his unwitting confession from actual rooms above or next to the main parlour in the Wise Woman's house. Conversely, the stage directions added in the present edition aim to emphasise the unlocalised quality of the Elizabethan and Jacobean stage, which allows the characters to witness Chartley's confessions while simply standing, unseen by Chartely or any other character, on the edge of the stage. For more details on the 'technical cleverness' (Verity, p. 251) of this scene, see Editor's Introduction on p. xiii.
19 *piece of work* the dress, but also Chartley himself, as indicated at 5.2.22, or the Wise Woman's piece of dramatic workmanship
28 *Gramercy* see 1.1.43
53 *lip labour* kiss
56 *putst finger in the eye* weep; proverbial (Tilley, F 229)
67 *grannam* see 2.1.176
75 *grannam* see 2.1.176
81 *gallant* of man, a fine gentleman; of a woman, as in this case, a

fashionably attired beauty

88 *post* see 4.4.90

89 *Rid out … Islington* the peculiar detour Chartley takes reflects the contemporary geography of the city and the areas immediately north of the City Wall. The seemingly quicker route from the city to Hoxton via Bishopsgate or Moorgate was not a viable option for a gentleman like Chartley. Stow explains that although ‘in the year 1415, the 3rd of Henry V, Thomas Fawconer, mayor, … caused the wall of the city to be broken toward the said moor (or fen), and built the postern called Moregate, for the ease of the citizens to walk that way upon causeys towards Iseldon and Hoxton’ (380), starting from 1527, ‘the further grounds beyond Finsbury Court [were] … overheightened with lay-stalls of dung’ (381). Stow also mentions the problem of enclosures: ‘the inhabitants of the towns about London, as Iseldon, Hoxton, Shoreditch and others, had so inclosed the common fields with hedges and ditches, that no Londoner ought to go out of the city, but in the highways’ (381). It is therefore hardly surprising that the gallant Chartley would choose to use the old fashionable highway, which ‘from Aldersgate, up to Iseldon, then on the right hand, turns east into Eald street’ and then on to Hoxton (383), rather than crossing a soiled area in pitch dark! See also Editor’s Introduction, p. xiv.

99 *dram* small drink of spirits

100 *turn up her heels* see 4.4.60-1

109 *nonplus* (to be in) a state of perplexity, or puzzle

111 *past grace* see *Dramatis Personae* 3

114-5 *more grace* see *Dramatis Personae* 3

117 *dotard* an imbecile, a stupid and foolish person

120 *proffers* offers

129 *Plots, plots* see 3.2.31 and 3.2.40

131 *to clear you* free you from doubt

139 *Heyday* expression of surprise

159-60 *rail of* more commonly, ‘rail at’, or ‘rail against’; use abusive

language against somebody, taunt, rant
165 *t'other* see 4.2.75
178-9 *neither … bachelor* See the Duke's line in Shakespeare's *Measure for Measure* 'Neither maid, widow nor wife' (5.1.178-9). Shakespeare's dark comedy was performed in 1604, which is also the probable date of the first performance of *The Wise Woman of Hoxton*.
180-1 *between … ground* proverbial (Tilley S 900)
185 *trot* see 2.1.40
trounce beat, thrash
192 *vagaries* whims, excesses, transgression from the norm
wag-pasty derogatory; a person likely to end up swinging from the hanger's noose
wild-oats see 2.1.116
203 *devil … dam* proverbial (Tilley D 225)
206 *good* clear
216 *ere* see 2.2.104
218 *grannam* see 2.1.176
235 *past grace* see *Dramatis Personae* 3
236 *retire* withdraw from former lifestyle
245 *more in me* what Chartley hears is an allusion to male genitals, while Luce 2 is obviously referring to her hidden female attributes
246-7 *mean forage* no longer attractive temptations
262-3 *an hand … an heart* see 3.3.113
267 *buss* kiss
274 *engross* monopolise, buy up wholesale

Commendatory Verse

5 *Mæcænas* Roman statesman and patron of the arts, who was born between 74BC and 64BC and died in 8BC. His famous literary circle included Horace and Virgil; his name has become synonymous with wealthy and generous patronage of the liberal

arts.

8 *lest* unless

15 *Atropos* one of the three Fates; Clotho spun the cord of human life, Lachesis measured it, and Atropos cut it. Death was therefore her 'office' (see line 16)

19 *Elysian* paradisal; from 'Elysium', in Greek mythology, the land inhabited by the blessed in afterlife

23 *Samuel King* A Clerkenwell neighbour and friend of Thomas Heywood

SYNOPSIS

The opening scene, which is set in a London "gaming-house", introduces the audience to one of the main characters in the play, the gallant Robin Chartley. He has been gambling his money away and refuses to stop playing until he has won his money back. Once he has recovered his losses, he starts questioning Sencer and Boyster about the women whose favours they plan to win. Gambling and courtship appear to be disturbingly similar activities in which the gentlemen clearly like to indulge. Sencer is happy to discuss his plan to woo Gratiana, Sir Harry's daughter, whereas Boyster is secretive and unwilling to disclose his feelings for Luce, the goldsmith's daughter. Boyster is unaware that Chartley is his rival. Boyster's laconic nature undermines his chances with Luce, who is clearly partial to Chartley's suave courtship and, more importantly, to his unabashed display of wealth and his promise of a comfortable life once they are married. Luce's father witnesses the exchange of vows between Chartley and his daughter and sets a date for the wedding. Chartley's only condition is that the wedding be kept secret until he comes of age because, he claims, his father might disinherit him should he find out that he has married without his consent. Thanks to the timely arrival of Luce 2, the audience realises that Chartley has an ulterior motive. His secrecy is due to his earlier engagement to Luce 2, a country gentlewoman, who, after being abandoned by Chartley the night before their wedding, has followed him to London disguised as a boy.

Chartley and Luce plan to get married at the Wise Woman's house in Hoxton. Prior to the celebration of their wedding, Luce 2 offers her services to the Wise Woman as a male servant called Jack, hoping to find a way of crossing Chartley's plans. Luce 2 is initiated to the secrets of the Wise Woman's profession. Although a charlatan, the Wise Woman is smart enough to trick her neighbours into believing that she does possess supernatural powers, such as 'forespeaking, … palmistry and recovering of things lost' (3.1.167-8). Her income, however, comes mainly from the letting of rooms to her "daughters" (prostitutes), whenever they happen to be "entertaining" a gentleman, and from providing shelter to pregnant unmarried women who wish to dispose of their babies before going back to their respectable households in London. When Luce 2 realises that Chartley is openly abusive to the Wise Woman, she suggests tricking Chartley into marrying her and Luce into marrying Boyster. The Wise Woman does not know that her male servant Jack is in fact the woman to whom Chartley had been previously contracted and agrees enthusiastically to go ahead with Jack's suggestion. Afraid that Chartley might realise that he has been cheated, the Wise Woman asks Luce and Jack (Luce 2) to swap their disguises. As a result, Boyster, who is legally married to Luce, is misled into thinking that he was the victim of a practical joke and believes himself "married" to a boy.

Sencer is similarly hindered in his pursuit of Gratiana both by lack of paternal consent and by Gratiana's openly hostile response to his advances. Undeterred by Gratiana's rejection, Sencer disguises himself as a scholar and outwits Sir Boniface in a mock contest which Sir Harry sets up in order to decide who is going to be appointed as Gratiana's tutor. His efforts fail to pay off once again, because Chartley, who believes himself a married man, is nevertheless determined to win Gratiana for himself. Chartley produces a forged letter, signed by his father, which pledges a 'jointure of three hundred pounds' (5.1.66-7) should Sir Harry agree to the match. Sir Harry, who deemed his daughter too young to marry at 2.2.52, welcomes the offer and sets a date for the wedding. When Luce hears that her wayward husband is about to marry another, she hurries to the Wise Woman to get her advice. Equally frustrated in their pursuit of Gratiana and Luce, Sencer and Boyster also go to the Wise Woman for help. The latter devises a clever plan to unmask Chartley before his victims, which functions as the comic denouement through which order and harmony are finally re-established.

The Wise Woman's plan consists in attracting all the injured parties to her house to witness Chartley's encounter with Luce, the woman whom he still believes to be his wife. Shown into rooms adjacent to the main parlour (see Glossarial Note at 5.2.11), Sir Harry, Gratiana, Boyster, and Old Chartley, who has with perfect comic timing arrived in London to look for his son, hear Chartley's unwitting confession and come out in turns to reproach him. The pairing off of the lovers and the final twist of Jack's disclosure of his/her real identity carry off elegantly, if improbably, the weight of the complex structure of this accomplished comedy.

TEXTUAL NOTES

The Wise-woman of Hogsdon was first published in 1638 by Henry Shepard, a publisher of plays and political tracts, who sold it at his shop in Chancery Lane at the sign of the Bible. The initials 'M.P.' on the title-page would suggest that the printer was Marmaduke Parsons, who had been appointed "master printer" by Star Chamber decree a year earlier.

Two compositors must have set type for the 1638 Quarto. The text clearly falls into two halves: sheets A – E, and sheets F - I. The two halves have variant running titles ('*Hogsdon*' in sheets A – E; '*Hogsden*' in sheets F – I) and distinctive spelling patterns ('Chartley' and 'Haringfield' in sheets A – E; 'Chartly' and 'Harringsfield' or 'Harings-field' in sheets F – I). The compositor who set the first, slightly longer half of the text, was clearly more competent: typographical mistakes are rare (see, for example, '*lacke*' as opposed to '*Iacke*' at C2r l.26). The second compositor was obviously less experienced. Acts 4 and 5, for example, appear as 'Actus 46' and 'Actus 56', probably because the compositor misread Heywood's usual abbreviations of 'quartus' (4s) and 'quintus' (5s) as '46' and '56'. Besides a significant number of typographical mistakes - 'feumd' (found) at H2v l.15; 'scene' (seen) at H4v l.8; '*wWiseoman*' (*Wisewoman*) at G4r l.1) - and turned letters - 'contrne' (construe) at F2r l.5; '*lingna*' (*lingua*) at F2r l.12; 'siun' (sin) at G3v l.27 - the second compositor failed to signal the end of Act 4, mispelt the Latin formula used in the first half of the play to signal the end of each act, and attributed a line spoken by Gratiana to a non-existent character called 'Anne'. Although speech-headings and stage directions were routinely normalised by the corrector in Parsons' printing shop who was in charge of preparing the copy for press, it is unlikely that such a blunder occurred in the authorial manuscript in the first place and then escaped the corrector's attention. It is far more likely that the compositor had difficulty reading his copy-text.

This edition is based on the four copies of the 1638 Quarto in the British Library (shelfmarks C.34.G.19(3); 644.e.41 (wants B2 and D4);

C.12.f.14(4) (wants I4); and Ashley 890). Press-variants among these copies occur in the outer formes of sheets G and I and in the inner forme of sheet F. The following list indicates readings from the corrected states of G(o), I(o) and F(i) as Qc, and readings from the uncorrected states as Qu. To the best of my knowledge, the only press variants to be recorded prior to this edition occur in the title and head-title of the copy at the Folger Shakespeare Library.

The following list records significant verbal emendations and departures from speech prefixes (SPs) and stage directions (SDs) in the 1638 Quarto (Q). Emendations and other departures from Q first introduced in this edition are followed by the abbreviation *this edn*. The other emendations and departures listed below originated in John Pearson's reprint (*Heywood's Dramatic Works*, vol. 5, 1874) and in A. W. Verity's edition (*Thomas Heywood, The Mermaid Series*, 1888), against which Q was checked. Although Pearson's 1874 is advertised as a reprint of the 1638 Quarto, some of its most obvious misprints are emended. Verity's edition expands the original stage directions and introduces the conventional act and scene division which is adopted in the present edition, except for Act 3 (See textual note 3.3.0 below).

This edition modernises the original spelling: 'Hogsdon/ Hogsden', 'Taber' and 'Saber', for example, are modernised for the fist time as 'Hoxton', 'Tabor' and 'Sabre'. 'And' in the sense of 'if' is spelt as 'an'. A few passages printed as prose in the 1638 Quarto are relined as verse and vice versa, although the peculiar blend of verse and prose which makes Heywood's style so fluid and versatile is carefully preserved. The constant shift between prose and verse is often suggestive of a change in register or of different modes of speech, as clearly illustrated by 3.2, where the earnest and pathetic expostulations in verse spoken by Luce and her father in 3.2 are interspersed by Chartley's cynical and self-interested replies in prose. The other formal features of the 1638 Quarto are faithfully preserved in this edition. Although the play is distinctive for its exuberant theatricality (see, for example, the complex blocking in 3.1 and 5.2, or Luce 2's double cross-dressing), the copy behind the 1638

Quarto was clearly prepared with a readerly audience in mind. The stage directions generously qualify character, status and locality, as the opening direction at the beginning of Act 5 shows: '*Enter* OLD MASTER CHARTLEY *as new come out of the country to inquire after his son, and three or four serving-men with blue coats to attend him*'. This direction provides further evidence that the copy for the 1638 Quarto was revised for the press and not for a revival on stage. The reference to '*three or four serving-men*' reflects an unwillingness to determine the exact number of non-speaking roles required by the play. The same tendency can be inferred from a discrepancy in the number of citizens' wives, which varies from two in the list of *Dramatis Personae* to four in the stage direction at the beginning of 2.1. While alerting its readers to this discrepancy in the glossarial notes, this edition refrains from emendation, on the grounds that other actors playing minor roles such as Joseph, Giles or Young Chartley's man could be used for doubling in this scene.

The decision to preserve the peculiar features of the 1638 Quarto edition is supported by the fact that Heywood might have prepared the copy of this play for press himself. Other plays written by Heywood earlier on in his career, such as *The Royal King and the Loyal Subject* (1602), *The Fair Maid of the West, Part I* (1604) and *The Iron Age, Parts I and II* (1612), were printed in the 1630s, when Heywood was becoming increasingly involved with some of the most prolific London printers and publishers. A substantial number of Heywood's early dramatic works are lost, probably because, as the Address to the Reader in *The Rape of Lucrece* (1608) suggests, although 'some have used a double sale of their labours, first to the Stage, and after to the presse', Heywood was 'ever faithfull in the first'. Although in 1633 Heywood was still claiming that 'my plays are not exposed unto the world in volumes, to bear the title of works (as others)', and that 'it never was any great ambition in me to be in this kind voluminously read' ('Address to the Reader', in *The English Traveller*, 1633, and 'Address to the Reader' in *The Fair Maid of the West, Part I*, 1631) shows a radical change in Heywood's attitude towards print culture. Heywood addresses his reader wishing that his plays may 'prove but as gratious in thy private reading, as they were plausible in the publick acting', thus overcoming the conflict of interests between the stage and the page as he had envisaged it in 1608. Starting from the early 1630s Heywood committed his works – mostly civic pageants – to the press straight after they were performed and he printed some of his earlier dramatic works, including *The Wise Woman of Hoxton*. He also supervised the printing of two copies owned by John Okes, *A Shoemaker a Gentleman* and *The Martyred Soldier*, both published in 1638.

Internal evidence supports the theory of Heywood's personal involvement with the printing of the 1638 Quarto of *The Wise Woman of Hoxton*. The above-mentioned stage direction at the beginning of 5.1 is 'distinctively authorial' (Dessen, 25). Further internal evidence is provided by the peculiar layout of the list of *Dramatis Personae*. None of the other plays printed by Marmaduke Parsons arranges the names of the characters in two adjacent columns. A similar layout appears in other dramatic works which were printed in the 1630s and which Heywood committed to the press himself, as intimated by the addresses to the readers signed by the author, such as *The Fair Maid of the West, Parts 1 and 2*. It is therefore likely that the layout in the 1638 Quarto reflects Heywood's own wish to map the fictive world of the play by arranging the characters' names into recognisable groups. The three young gallants Chartley, Sencer and Boyster, who will get married at the end of the play, open the first column. Luce and the Wise Woman, whose friendship can hardly be explained without calling Luce's spotless virtue into question, are teasingly placed on the same line across the two columns. Luce and Gratiana are placed alongside the members of their respective households, whereas Old Master Chartley, who represents a central figure of authority in the fictive world of the play, is placed close to the bottom of the first column. Unlike the Victorian editor, who arranges the characters according to gender and social status, with the male characters preceding the female, and the masters preceding their servants, this edition acknowledges the significance of the original list and therefore preserves it as it appeared in the 1638 Quarto.

Dramatis Personae

1 ROBIN] *this edn; not in* Q
5 TABOR] *this edn; Taber* Q (*modernised throughout*)
9 HOXTON] *this edn; Hogsdon/Hogsden* Q (*modernised throughout*)
14 *who*] *this edn; that* Q
16-7 LUCE *2 … gentlewoman*] *this edn*; The second LUCE *Verity*; *not in* Q
17 *Chartley's … gentleman*] *this edn; not in* Q
18 SERVING-MAN 1, SERVING-MAN 2] *this edn; not in* Q
19 *Gratiana's man*] *this edn; not in* Q
20 GILES] *this edn; not in* Q

1.1

7 another] *Verity*; an other Q
11 up] *Pearson;* tp Q
18 *aside*] *Verity*; *not in* Q
26 *aside*] *this edn; not in* Q
41 SD] *this edn; not in* Q
43 *cinques*] *Verity*; Sinks Q
50 SD] *this edn; Chartley throwes out* (*at line* 49) Q
Todo] *Verity*; To tho Q
52 SD] *this edn; not in* Q
65 SD] *line* 66 *in* Q
118 hath … , as] *this edn;* hath, as Q
119 do.] *this edn*; do; &c. Q (&c. *might suggest something too bawdy for print*)
129 *aside*] *this edn*; *not in* Q
134 SP] *Pearson*; Sencer Q
135 SD] *this edn; Exit Sencer* Q (*after line* 135)

158	SD] *Verity*; *Exeunt* Q

1.2

1.2.0.2	*apprentice*] *this edn; Prentice* Q
62	SD] *this edn; not in* Q
75	SD] *this edn; not in* Q
76	*aside*] *this edn*; *not in* Q
77	SD] *this edn; not in* Q
79	*aside*] *this edn; not in* Q
112	*aside*] *Verity; not in* Q
116	*Dædalus*'s] *Verity*; *Dædalus his* Q
132	an] *this edn*; *and* Q
	SD] *this edn; not in* Q
134	SD LUCE'S FATHER] *this edn; her Father* Q
135	on] *this edn; of* Q
138 ff.	SP] *this edn; Father.* Q
140	*aside*] *Verity*; *not in* Q
153-4	SD] *this edn; not in* Q
155	SD] *this edn; not in* Q
156-7	SD] *this edn; not in* Q
157	Ah] *this edn; Ha* Q
159-60	SD] *this edn; not in* Q
188	*aside*] *Verity*; *not in* Q
199	SD] *Verity*; *Exeunt* Q
216	SD] *Verity; Exit. Explicit Actus primus* Q

2.1

2.1.0.2	*four women like citizens' wives* see Textual Notes, p. 133
2.1.0.3	KITCHEN MAID] *Verity; Chamber-mayd* Q

1 SD] *this edn; not in* Q
5 SD] *this edn; not in* Q
6 SD *unseen*] *this edn*; *stands aside* Q; *in Boy's clothes; she stands aside, Verity*
14 *aside*] *Verity; not in* Q
27 Coldharbour] *this edn; Coleharbour* Q
39 *aside*] *this edn; not in* Q
44 SD] *Verity; not in* Q
86 SD] *Verity; not in* Q
88 *aside*] *Verity; not in* Q
93 *aside*] *Verity; not in* Q
97 *aside*] *this edn; not in* Q
102 *aside*] *this edn; not in* Q
105 SD HARINGFIELD *and* CHARTLEY,] *this edn;* Haringfield, *and* Chartley Q
116 *aside*] *Verity; not in* Q
161 *aside*] *this edn; not in* Q
180 SD] *this edn; not in* Q

2.2

18 SD] *this edn; not in* Q
43 *aside*] *this edn; not in* Q
66 Mitre] *Verity; Miter in* Q
91 *aside*] *Verity; not in* Q
120 tabor] *Verity; Taber* Q
121 SD] *this edn; not in* Q
127 SD] *Verity; not in* Q
158 SD] *Verity; not in* Q
163 SD] *this edn; Enter a pedanticall Schoolmaster, Sir* Boniface Q
181 *aside*] *this edn; not in* Q
183 *verum*] *vero* Q

201 *et*] *Verity; &* Q
214 your] *Verity; you* Q
216 physiognomy] *Verity;* Phisnomy Q
221 that] *this edn; yet* Q
224 Magnus] *this edn; Magnes* Q
229 SD] *Verity; not in* Q
236 SD] *Verity; Exeunt. Explicit Actus secundus.* Q

3.1

3.1.0.1 *disguised … Jack*] *this edn; which was* Iack *in woman's apparell* Q
41 *aside*] *Verity; not in* Q
51 *aside*] *Verity; not in* Q
77 SD] *Verity; not in* Q
84 *aside*] *this edn; not in* Q
88 *aside*] *this edn; not in* Q
101 SD *severally*] *Verity; at severall places* Q
106 SD] *this edn; not in* Q
107 SD] *this edn; Meaning* Boyster Q
110 SD] *this edn; not in* Q
111-2 SD] *this edn; not in* Q
116 SD] *this edn; not in* Q
117 SD] *this edn; not in* Q
120 SD LUCE 2] *this edn; Iack* Q
133 Boniface's] *Verity; Boniface his* Q
136 SD] *this edn; not in* Q
138 SD *Luce 2 … Luce*] *Verity; and others* Q
140 SD CHARTLEY *and* BOYSTER] *this edn; not in* Q
145 *aside*] *this edn; not in* Q
149 they] *this edn; not in* Q
153 SD] *Verity; not in* Q
154 SD] *Verity; not in* Q

3.2

3.2.0.1	SD *Master*] *this edn; not in* Q
12	SD *unmasking*] *this edn; halfe ready and maskt* Q
13	*aside*] *this edn; not in* Q
16	*aside*] *this edn; not in* Q
18	*aside*] *this edn; not in* Q
33	I shall] *this edn; I'se* Q
38	SD] *Verity; not in* Q

3.3

3.3.0	Scene Division] *this edn; Verity continues from 3.2*
3.3.0.1	SD *severally*] *this edn; not in* Q
	SD SERVING-MAN 1] *this edn; his man* Q
24	SD SERVING-MAN 2] *this edn; a serving-man* Q
29	SD] *Verity (and* Serving-man*); Exit* Q
32	SD] *Verity; not in* Q
35	SP] *this edn; Servingman* Q
35	SD] *Verity; not in* Q
87	SD LUCE'S FATHER] *this edn; her Father.* Q
135	life] *Verity; like* Q
154	*aside*] *this edn; not in* Q
162	in] *Verity;* , no Q
171	latter] *Verity;* later Q
185	SD] *Verity; not in* Q
188	*aside*] *this edn; not in* Q
197	*aside*] *this edn; not in* Q
202	*aside*] *this edn; not in* Q
203	not] *Verity; not in* Q

213	SD] *this edn; Exit* Q
217	I'm] *this edn;* I am Q
244	SD *Exit*] *Verity; Exeunt. Explicit Actus tertius* Q

4.1

4.1.0.1	*Enter* …GRATIANA] *this edn; Enter …Gratiana, with others.* Q
4.1.0.1 ff	SD HARINGFIELD] *Verity; Harringsfield or Harings-field used alternatively in* Q (*see* Textual Notes, p. 131)
20	SD] *this edn; not in* Q
51	Brasenose] *this edn; Brazen nose* Q
67	*Nominativo*] *Verity; Nomnativo* Q
69	*construe*] *Verity; consterue* Q
70	construe] *Verity; constrne* Q
78	Μουσοτροφος] *this edn;* Moosotropos Q
	ποετες] *this edn;* poetatis Q
79	ρετωρ] *this edn;* retoon Q
	ουχ] *this edn;* onch Q
	ελαχιστε] *this edn;* elashiste Q
	σοφων] *this edn;* sophoon Q
80	*materna lingua*] *Verity; maternal lingna* Q
86	himself] *Verity; him* Q
91	*numquam*] *Verity; nunquam* Q
102	*ego sum*] *Verity; egosum* Q
117	Di – cunt] *this edn; Di –* Q
124	is it] *this edn; it is* Q
	make] *Verity;* makes Q
145	SD] *this edn; at line* 146-7 *in* Q
149	SD] *this edn; not in* Q
161	SD] *this edn; not in* Q
168	fetched] *Verity;* fetch Q
169	SD] *Verity; Exit* Q

172	SD] *Verity; at line* 173 *in* Q
176	SD *carrying a letter*] *this edn; in his hand a Lady* Q; *with Gratiana, Verity*
176 ff.	SD CHARTLEY] *Verity; Chartly* Q (*see* Textual Notes, p. 131)
178-9	SD] *Verity; not in* Q
183	*aside*] *this edn; not in* Q
195	SD] *Verity; not in* Q
206	*aside*] *Verity; not in* Q
214	till] *Verity*; tell Q
216	*aside*] *this edn; not in* Q
223	SD] *this edn; not in* Q
226	T'endow] *this edn;* To endowe Q
231	off] *Verity; of* Q
235	SD *all but* SENCER] *Verity; not in* Q
241	scorn] *Pearson;* Horne Q

4.2

9	me?] *this edn;* mee. Q
19	SD] *this edn; not in* Q
26	*aside*] *this edn; not in* Q
31	SD] *this edn; not in* Q
40	bridesmaid] *this edn;* Bride maid Q
48	Street.] Qc; streete Qu
54	within] Qu; within, Qc
55	echoing] Qu; ecchoing Qc
58	untruth,] Qc; untruth Qu
63	SD] *this edn; not in* Q
65	*holds* SD] *Verity; held* Q
75	*aside*] *this edn; not in* Q
79	SD] *this edn; not in* Q
81	*aside*] *this edn; not in* Q

85 swoon] *this edn;* swound Q
90 *aside*] *this edn; not in* Q
94 SD] *this edn; not in* Q
95 SD] *this edn; not in* Q
98 let] *Verity;* call Q
107 *too*] *Verity; two* Q
113 SP LUCE] *Pearson; continues to* LUCE'S FATHER (*Father.*) *in* Q
SP LUCE'S FATHER] *Pearson; attributed to Luce. in* Q
120 SP] *Pearson; continues to* LUCE'S FATHER (*Father.*) *in* Q
138 yet] Qc; yet. Qu

4.3

5 looming] Qu; Looming Qc
fortune] Qu; Fortune Qc
7 SD] *this edn; not in* Q
8 Who's] *Verity;* Whose Q
11 belike] Qc; be like Qu
14 SD] *this edn; not in* Q
19 SD] *this edn; not in* Q
20 in,] Qc; in Qu
SD] *Verity; Exit* Q
24 on] *Verity; not in* Q
27 *aside*] *this edn; not in* Q
32 can] *this edn;* and you Q
34 SD *and* LUCE 2] *this edn; not in* Q
38 *aside*] *this edn; not in* Q
me!] Qc; mee. Qu
40 wife] *Verity; not in* Q
44 SD] *this edn; not in* Q
46 *aside*] *this edn; not in* Q
53 set] *Verity*; sell Q

53	SD *Master*] *this edn; not in* Q
55	An] *this edn;* And Q
57	SD] *this edn; not in* Q
60	SD] *this edn; not in* Q
65	then] *this edn;* them Q; thou, *Verity*
66	truce] *Verity;* trince Q
67	hear't] *this edn;* heare it Q
68	SD] *this edn; not in* Q
69	SD] *this edn; not in* Q
71	SD] *this edn*; *not in* Q
72	SD] *this edn; not in* Q
74	SD] *this edn; not in* Q
76	SD] *this edn; not in* Q
78	SD] *this edn; not in* Q
	her] *this edn;* him Q
78-9	SD] *this edn; not in* Q
79-80	SD] *this edn; not in* Q
81	SD] *this edn; not in* Q
86	wise] *Pearson;* wiser Q
	SD] *Verity; Exit* Q

4.4

4.4.0.1-2	SD] *this edn; Enter* Taber *and sir* Boniface *with a Trencher, with broken meat and a Napkin* Q
7	Sabre] *this edn;* Saber Q
11	SD *disguised*] *this edn; not in* Q
25	SD] *Verity; at line 27 in* Q
26	our] *Verity;* your Q
31	off,] Qu; off Qc
35	*manos*] *this edn*; *manus* Q
36	*À votre service*] *this edn; A vostre servitor* Q

37 Ha] *this edn;* Hee Q
41 Master] *Verity;* Mr Q
51 SD] *this edn; Exeunt Sir Boniface and Haringfield, Verity; not in* Q
53 dear,] Qc; deere Qu
55 contents] Qc; contente Qu
56 *aside*] *this edn; not in* Q
59 SD] *this edn; not in* Q
62 SD] *this edn; Hee reades* Q
94 SD] *this edn; not in* Q
95 SD] *Verity; not in* Q
111 *aside*] *Verity; not in* Q
114 *aside*] *Verity; not in* Q
117 SD] *this edn; not in* Q
120 *aside*] *Verity; not in* Q
122 *aside*] *Verity; not in* Q
123 travail] *this edn;* travel Q
124 *aside*] *Verity; not in* Q
146 buy] *Verity;* by Q
152 your] *this edn;* you Q; *this half line is attributed to Sencer in Verity*

5.1

5.1.0.2 *three or four serving-men* see Textual Notes, p. 133
20 found] *Pearson;* feumd Q
64 SD] *Verity (at line* 63); *not in* Q
101 th'intruding] *this edn;* the intruding Q

5.2

5.2.0.1 SD *disguised*] *this edn; not in* Q
5.2.0.2 LUCE'S FATHER] *this edn; her* Father Q

8 SD] *this edn; not in* Q
9 *aside*] *this edn; not in* Q
12 SD] *this edn; They withdraw. Exeunt* Wise-woman *and 2nd* LUCE, *Verity; Exeunt* Q
SD *while … right*] *this edn; not in* Q
14 Ever] *this edn; at line* 13 *in* Q
17 SD] *this edn; not in* Q
24 SD] *this edn; not in* Q
26 SD *Exit* WISE WOMAN] *this edn; not in* Q
SD *while … left*] *this edn;* GRATIANA *withdraws, exeunt the others, Verity; not in* Q
33 SD] *this edn; not in* Q
35 SD] *this edn; not in* Q
37 SD] *this edn; not in* Q
42 seen] *Pearson*; scene Q
45 SD OLD CHARTLEY *sits …*] *this edn; Takes him into one of the inner rooms, Verity; not in* Q
SD *Enter …*] *this edn; not in* Q
48 SD] *this edn; not in* Q
51 SD *Exit … at the other*] *this edn; Exeunt* SENCER *and* Wise-woman, *Verity; not in* Q
SD *… who then exits*] *this edn; who retires, Verity; not in* Q
54 *aside*] *this edn; In an inner room, Verity; not in* Q
aside] *this edn; In another inner room, Verity; not in* Q
aside] *this edn; Also in an inner room, Verity; not in* Q
58 SP] *Verity; Anne* Q
59 *aside*] *this edn; not in* Q
61 *aside*] *this edn; not in* Q
62 *aside*] *Verity; not in* Q
66 *aside*] *this edn; not in* Q
67 *aside*] *Verity; not in* Q
aside] *In an inner room, Verity; not in* Q
73 *aside*] *this edn; not in* Q

74 *aside*] *this edn; not in* Q
aside] *this edn; not in* Q
75 *aside*] *this edn; not in* Q
83 *aside*] *Verity; not in* Q
91 *aside*] *Verity; not in* Q
aside] *this edn; not in* Q
93 *aside*] *this edn; not in* Q
102 SD] *this edn; Coming from the inner room, Verity; not in* Q
123 *Gratiana*] *Grat. Verity; Grace* Q
126 SD] *this edn; Enter* Sir HARRY, *at line* 139 *in Verity; not in* Q
Vile] *Verity;* Vil'd Q
138 SD] *this edn; Enter* Old CHARTLEY, *at line* 140 *in Verity; not in* Q
145 SP] *Pearson; Chart.* Q
152 *aside*] *this edn; not in* Q
154 SD] *this edn; Enter* BOYSTER, *at line* 155 *in Verity; not in* Q
161 I'll] *Pearson;* He Q
167 SD] *this edn; Enter* LUCE'S Father, *at line* 168 *in Verity; not in* Q
178 widower] *Verity;* widdow Q
192 of this] *Pearson;* of this, of this Q
wild-oates] *Pearson;* wil-doates Q
200 th'inconstant] *this edn;* the inconstant Q
201 give] *Verity;* gave Q
205 SD] *Verity; not in* Q
206 the] *Pearson;* then Q
209 After, she] *this edn*; After she Q
217 SD] *this edn; not in* Q
227 regard] *Pearson*; regarded Q
235 grace] *Verity; Grace* Q
246-47 mean forage] *this edn;* meane forige Q; foreign, *Pearson and Verity*
247 SD] *this edn; not in* Q
252 *Scattering her hair*] *this edn;* shee skatters her hayre. (*continues from line* 252) Q

268 SD] *this edn; not in* Q
276 SD *Exeunt all*] *this edn; Exeunt omnes. Explicat Actus 56*. Q
FINIS] *this edn; after Commendatory Verse in* Q

Commendatory Verse

8 lest] *this edn;* lesse Q

Reference Sources

Berger, Thomas L. and William C. Bradford, Jr., *An Index of Characters in English Printed Drama to the Restoration* (Englewood, Colorado: Microcard Editions Books, 1975)

Dessen, A., *Elizabethan Stage Conventions and Modern Interpreters* (Cambridge: Cambridge University Press, 1984)

Harbage, A., S. Schoenbaum and S. S. Wagonheim, *Annals of English Drama: 975-1700* (London and New York: Routledge, 1989)

King, T. J., *Casting Shakespeare's Plays: London Actors and Their Roles, 1590-1642* (Cambridge: Cambridge University Press, 1992)

Kökeritz, H., *Shakespeare's Pronunciation* (New Haven: Yale University Press, 1953)

Partridge, E., *Shakespeare's Bawdy* (London: Routledge, 1968)

Rubinstein, F., *A Dictionary of Shakespeare's Sexual Puns and their Significance* (London: Macmillan, 1984)

Sugden, E. H., *A Topographical Dictionary to the Works of Shakespeare and his Fellow Dramatists* (Manchester: Manchester the University Press, 1925)

Tilley, M.P., *A Dictionary of the Proverbs in England in the Sixteenth and Seventeenth Century* (Ann Arbor: University of Michigan Press, 1950)

Walker, T. A., *A Biographical Register of Peterhouse Men* (Cambridge: Cambridge University Press, 1930)

Wheatley, H. B. (ed.), *Stow's Survey of London* (London and New York: Dent and Dutton, 1912)

Facsmile of The Wise-Woman of Hogsdon (London, 1638), fol.A2.
Reproduced by permission of The British Library (C.34.g.19.(3))

THE WISE-WOMAN OF HOGSDON.

Actus primus, Scena prima.

Enter, as newly come from play, foure young Gentlemen,
Master Chartley, *Master* Sencer, *M.* Boyster
and Master Haringfield.

Chartley.

PRice of my life: now if the Devill have bones,
these Dyce are made of his. Was ever such a
cast seene in this Age? Could any Gull in Europe
(saving my selfe) fling such a cast?

Boyster. Eye. *Chart.* No.

Boyster. Yes.

Chart. But I say no: I have lost an hundred pound,
And I will have my saying.

Boyst. I have lost an other hundred, Ile have mine.
Ey, yes, I flung a worse: a worse by oddes.

Chart. I cry you mercy sir, loosers may speake,
Ile not except 'gainst you: but let me see
Which of these two that pocket up our Cash
Dares contradict me?

Sencer. Sir, not I:
I say you have had bad casting.

Haring. So say I.

Chart. I say this Hatt's not made of wooll;
Which of you all dares say the contrary?